WHO ARE YOU BECOMING?
BLESSED AND UNSTOPPABLE

JOHN HUNTER

Produced by Street Media and Publishing, LLC
St. Petersburg, FL | Dallas, TX

FOREWORD

by Cindie Buchanon

Open your heart and mind to *Who are You Becoming? Blessed and Unstoppable.* Why? The author, drawing on his own life story, is presenting you, the reader, with a straightforward roadmap to becoming the best version of you. Who doesn't want that?

John artfully uses his life story to illustrate how you, no matter how broken you may believe yourself to be, can use the power within yourself to evolve into a new you, a better you—more compassionate, more self-confident, more filled with love and gratitude.

In his book, John provides his readers with a blueprint to begin their journey—to a become the best version of themselves. All that is required is the sincere desire to change—to prepare an action plan; to identify your limiting beliefs (those that are holding you back from dreaming and achieving goals); to take inventory of the reasons/excuses you habitually use to avoid pursuing your goals and dreams; to actively shift and reset your daily mindset when it fails to align with your action plan; and, most importantly, to actively engage in your action plan.

John identifies and describes the strategies/methods he found fundamental to his journey—using a daily journal to record thoughts, hopes, dreams, obstacles; completing a Life Wheel, ranking oneself in terms of finances, relationships, etc., and employing a professional coach.

John's book is filled with what I describe as pearls of wisdom. Among them are: acknowledge and accept that neither your circumstances nor your past defines you; honor your past but don't give it permission to haunt you; the most important relationship you will ever have in your life is with yourself; gratitude begins as

5

an internal journey; we grow far more from pain and failure than we ever will from success; and, lastly, you're leaving your mark on the world, whether you realize it or not.

I am a personal friend of John's and a long-time colleague. I have written my share of technical "how-to" books. I am a reader of fiction and non-fiction alike and have read my share of self-help books. I am pleased to note that I have rarely read a self-help book that so remarkably captures the author's passion and dedication to helping others. John's strategies for interpersonal transformation are not only grounded in his personal experience but they are strategies that anyone can implement in their daily lives. I have been privileged and enlightened to read and contemplate the blueprint of John's journey and how his readers can learn from his struggles and apply what he learned to their own lives.

Inspiration may be taken from this last "pearl." It's all about taking action. Mindset is only half of the battle. You still have to put in the work.

ACKNOWLEDGMENTS

My father, John R. Hunter, thank you for always listening and never judging me. You are a walking example of what a good Christian man looks like. I love you.

My mother, Shirley Barnett, you are one of a kind. Thanks for always keeping me accountable with my faith. You are a strong, Beautiful woman of God.

My sister, Sheri Snyder, thank you for your unconditional love and support. I appreciate you so much. You are truly Blessed and Unstoppable.

My counselor, Tom Edwards, thanks for helping me through the toughest time in my life. We had some real hard talks. You are a great guy.

My friends, Bob and Cindie Buchanon, wow! what can I say. You are like my parents, my role models, my family. I owe you so much, you both mean the world to me. Love you guys.

My mentor, Daniel Feliciano, my buddy, my mentor, my role model, my friend… You mean more to me than I could ever explain. Thank you for being a strong, bold man of God. Thank you for our talks. Thank you for praying for me. You and your incredible wife are strong role models whom my wife and I will aim to be like. Love you buddy.

My wife, Lacole Foster Hunter, WOW!!!!!!! What we have been through together and apart is Life changing. You have taught me so much, babe. My love grows deeper and deeper for you each and every day. I honor you for the rest of my life. My Queen forever. Guess what babe? We did it!! I love you.

Thanks also to my editor and publisher Daphne Taylor Street with Street Media and Publishing, LLC for making this book a reality and to my proofreader Teresa Cundiff for helping straighten out the many little details.

Table of Contents

INTRODUCTION

"10 Finally, be strong in the Lord and in his mighty power. 11 Put on the full armor of God, so that you can take your stand against the devil's schemes."

—Ephesians 6:10,11

Dear Readers,

Thank you for joining me on this journey as I present my first book to you. I'll keep this introduction short and simple so that we can dive straight into the heart of why I wrote this book in the first place—this book is my gift to you.

The road that led me to the place I am now, having written this book, has been long and arduous. The various maps I've used to lead me along the way have been worn out, faded, re-drawn, discarded, replaced for newer versions, and torn to shreds in frustration many times over. So much frustration, until I realized that the journey and the destination has been in God's hands all along, never mine. He has plotted a much better course for me than anything I could have imagined, and I've finally learned to trust it. Moving forward, God has control over the map, and I'm here in service, humbly and respectfully, for you.

No matter what your personal beliefs about God might be, this book is a manifestation of my journey, as I share my personal life stories with you, coupled with the lessons I've learned from it all. My intention and hope is that it might inspire, uplift, motivate, and mostly help you discover specific actions that you can take to get more out of your own life, fulfill more of your own goals and dreams, and provide tools and tips that can propel you on your own journey.

Thank you for joining me, and I invite you to connect with me if my words touch or impact you in some way. You can reach me through my website or social media, and you can even book me for a speaking engagement for your corporate event, seminar, or class—wherever I can serve to inspire, motivate, and spread positivity. I look forward to hearing from you.

Let the journey commence…

CHAPTER 1: Becoming Your Best YOU

The most interesting people that I've ever met or known about in my life have experienced extraordinary hardship in their lives. They've fallen to painful depths in life, and they lifted themselves up, emerging a little wiser, a little more compassionate and with a fire in them to achieve greater things—to be extraordinary. There is nothing wrong with being ordinary; that's great! There are many, many wonderful ordinary people in the world who are beloved and deeply valued. However, to be extraordinary, to be different from most, it takes something extra: extra work, extra focus, extra heart, extra grace, extra courage, and extra faith. That's what makes someone extra-ordinary.

I'm also going to make a prediction, and my prediction is that if you are reading this book, there is a 99% chance that you, too, have faced extraordinary hardship in your life—you've suffered and struggled. Maybe your life has gone down some unpleasant paths or just took several wrong turns, and you've emerged wiser, more compassionate and you have a fire within you to achieve greater things. If that's true, and if you are seeking a life that is far more extraordinary than what you're experiencing now, if you want to be different, a person of purpose, inspiration, and success in all areas of your life, then I'm here to tell you that you can be that person. In fact, you are already that person. You just have to put in the work to peel down those layers that aren't serving you and focus on who you are becoming—the extraordinary version of you that you are meant to be.

Whatever you've gone through in your life, whatever self-doubt and unworthiness might be penetrating your thoughts, whatever mistakes you have made or circumstances have knocked you down, these are not your barriers. These are your fuel to power you up, igniting the spark inside of you to create the extraordinary self you dream to be. I'm so confident that this is an absolute fact for you because it is not only the blueprint of my journey, but it's the same blueprint for almost all extraordinary men and women throughout history and today. Martin Luther King, Jr., Maya Angelou, Anthony Robbins, Lisa Nichols, Steve Harvey, Malala Yousafzai and countless others have charged through the hardships they faced in their lives and emerged with a fire which they have used to empower others. Would they have been so extraordinary if their lives had been easy? Would they be memorable if they hadn't used their pain to fuel their life's purpose? I'll let you seek out your own answers to these questions, and through searching, you'll find the truth that speaks to your heart. I know what I believe.

Your Journal

This book is specifically designed to engage you in your search while providing some insights, action steps and opportunities to take a deep dive into your own thoughts, wants and actions. For best results, please designate a journal to use as your companion as you journey through this book. It can be a special journal or just a designated pad of paper, but this book is designed for you to actively use right now to guide you on your path as you design a more purposeful, blessed and unstoppable you.

At the end of each chapter, you will come across "Take Action Now" sections, providing exercises, tips and action steps that when used, will create an interactive experience with the lessons from the chapters. In some sections, you'll create lists or to write down your thoughts on certain subjects along with other activities. However, I also encourage you to journal from your own mind and heart as you're reading and processing the content in each chapter. Consider how elements from the chapter pertain to your life now, what you think about what you read and how the stories and tips might have impacted your thoughts and feelings as you were reading. Write about what you're processing in your mind and heart. This will allow you to delve deeper into yourself making this book a highly personal and impactful experience for you.

My Story

Throughout this book, you'll learn about my personal journey as I worked to become the man I am today. I'm sharing this with you mostly because when we share our stories, we create a deeper connection with one another and we recognize the similarities we

17

each experience through being human. Plus, it's an easy way to see how the lessons and activities presented in this book have a direct impact on personal development when applied. I'm living proof, and I promise you that I walk the walk. Everything that I teach, coach and recommend, I do myself. These action steps have been profoundly transformative for me and countless others which is why this book exists.

I was raised in a good home with strong Christian values and faith, but despite having a loving and strong family, I believed that I was stupid and worthless most of my life. These weren't baseless feelings. I mean, I failed kindergarten. Who fails kindergarten? A stupid kid—me—I did. My siblings were brilliant, accomplished, with good grades and notable achievement all throughout their lives. I was a complete disappointment. Everyone was too kind to say that to my face, but I felt it just by the way no one expected anything from me. I endured the cruelty of other kids and even sexual abuse during that time. Then, in my youth, I ended up in jail facing a crime that left me feeling terrified and ostracized from most of "normal" society. I was even afraid to apply for a "normal" job. Not only were the outward consequences frightening and humiliating, but it pained me to think about what this said about who I was, the picture it painted of me and the monster, depraved degenerate other people were going to think I was when they would find out.

There's more to this story, of course, and the following chapters will not only reveal these stories to you, but they are attached to those lessons I mentioned earlier on—how you emerge from the hardships you survive and overcome, with some wisdom, drive and success when you make it through to the other side. I allowed the pain from my past to fuel my fire to become different, to transform myself and to live a life of purpose… for you. Every day, it is my greatest gift to be able to love, support and inspire others to be the best version of themselves that they dream to be.

That's what drove me to write this book. If someone like me, who failed kindergarten and made it through many other hardships— I'm just an ordinary guy—if I can transform my life to be blessed and unstoppable, I know for a fact that you can, too. So, it was important for me to share this story, to reach even more people with this message. I'm not Martin Luther King, Jr., Steve Harvey, or Anthony Robbins, and I don't need to be them. I'm John Hunter, and I am someone who decided that I must use the life that God gave me to be different for you, to help inspire, to coach, and to offer decisive action steps that can help guide you on your own journey to become your extraordinary you.

Transformation Power

One day, I had a massive revelation while sitting in my office speaking with a woman who was telling me about her daughter, and she told me that her daughter really needed my coaching services and asked if I would help her. Of course, I said yes, and I would be honored to do so, but something in me lit up about the wild irony of this request. Although I hope it didn't show outwardly, inside my head, my mouth was gaped open wide when the enormity of this scenario hit hard.

Seriously, I was the guy mothers warned their daughters about—I was the guy moms feared that their daughters would meet. I was a sly, smooth, good looking exotic dancer, and I was definitely a womanizer. Nearly every woman was a sexual interest to me years ago, and now, today, in the wake of extreme personal growth and transformation, this mom told me that she intuitively knew that her daughter needed my life coaching services. Wow! That's the power of a true positive life transformation.

A part of me, remembering my former self thought: but I'm a wolf. Why would you bring your daughter to a wolf? Of course, I know why. I'm not a wolf anymore. Seriously, that way of thinking doesn't even cross my mind any longer, to the extent that I don't even recognize the person that I once was, his values and actions. However, I'm still fully aware that I was that person once and to have someone trust me like this is an incredible and humbling

19

feeling. It was a testament to how far I've actually come on my journey.

I'm so far divorced from my former self today that it's actually a little funny. I have a few friends who will say, "Man, you never want to go out; you never want to do anything."

Well, their idea of "going out" and "doing anything" is usually going to bars and hitting on women, etc. That's nothing I'm interested in doing anymore. I recall a time when a friend was trying to get me to go to Vegas. He was saying, "Hey, it's just us guys, man. Just going to have fun, you know?" Honestly, there's nothing there that interests me, and I'm dead serious. There's nothing about that idea that makes me want to go. I'm just so far removed from wanting anything that hanging out in Vegas with the guys has to offer. I don't drink; I don't gamble, and I'm not interested in picking up random women, so what would I do there?

Seriously, my obsession now is on mindset and self-growth, and this is my life. So, if I met a woman during this Vegas trip, I'd only sit with her and talk about my coaching and what I do, and the power of mindset and personal development, and what does she do for a living… I just wouldn't fit in! Now, if we were going to Vegas for a personal development conference, that I could do. We weren't on the same page, so I passed.

Get Unstuck

One of the key factors in personal transformation is working your way out of the mindset of "feeling stuck." Feeling stuck is a trap, and most often—not always—it's a trap within your own mind that holds you captive because it's been your reality for too long. Feeling stuck is so ingrained in your consciousness that it can be difficult to imagine anything else. The key to this is understanding that your circumstances do not define you. You can behave differently, take different actions, develop a different mindset and change your circumstances. We all get stuck—I was stuck in a

20

mindset believing that I was stupid, that I was a womanizer and that I was worthless. At times I'd lift myself out of these traps, but I'd find myself falling right back into them with the old narratives looping in my head that I don't deserve to be different, that I was only pretending to be someone better than who I really was. That's staying stuck!

No one—not me, not you, not your loved ones—no one needs to stay stuck. No one is doomed to remain being someone they don't want to be. You not only have the power within you to evolve in to a new you, but you must realize that this is a critical change for you to make so that the world can experience the best you possible. Your loved ones, your kids, your spouse, your friends, your colleagues and clients, even strangers will all be blessed when you show up as the best version of you possible. Don't cheat them of that when you have the power to change, but most importantly, don't cheat yourself. I speak from experience—this is the best life that I have ever lived, and I've had some wild times! Nothing compares to living a life filled with purpose, gratitude and love.

Building Self-worth

If you don't believe that you're meant for more, you won't do more. This is easier said than done when you're feeling low, I know. How to get started can be challenging because with self-doubt comes all of the voices in your head telling you that you're unworthy, you don't deserve confidence, you're worthless, you shouldn't trust yourself, etc. The key is finding a place to start building your self-worth. I recommend focusing on the little things that you know give you a sense of empowerment or achievement. For me, my faith in God was my starting point. He created me, and therefore, He has a plan for me, which is greater than any plan I might have for myself. I turned my power over to God, and I let Him use me for His will for me.

Of course, you don't need to use faith as your starting point—that's just my example. Begin with the people in your life who love

21

you, the things you're good at doing, the people you make smile or who make you feel valued. There are so many people struggling with depression and anxiety, and at the center of it all, you're going to find a person who is struggling with self-worth and missing direction or purpose to drive them in a way that's meaningful to them. It doesn't matter where you've been or what you've been through—your worthiness is not determined by your circumstances. Your worthiness is determined by whether you stick around and show up to make your next move, even if it's hard, even if it's slow, even when it seems impossible.

If you have purpose, and you have a solid sense of self-worth, it's much easier to get through depression, anxiety, conflicts or just bad days. You can push forward, and all bad days eventually come to an end—that's literally how bad days work.

There's also a bit of caution that I need to offer up about self-worth, too. This is about the potential of appearances versus substance. It's not too difficult to fake a sense of self-worth, and there's nothing wrong with faking it to get through tough times when the real thing is too difficult to access. However, that's not sustainable, and it isn't real. Dig deep and look at the actions you take in your life. Then ask yourself: is this what someone with real self-worth would do? Are you doing the things that someone who believes in him or herself would do? Are you taking the action steps to prove that you believe in yourself?

Grabbing this book, reading it, then taking the action steps listed in it is a solid start, and that's another reason I wanted to write this book and have it available to you. It's about taking actions that both drive and reflect your self-worth. If you really believe that you are worth more, then the actions you take would prove it.

Using This Book

The most important thing I'll ask of you is to not just passively read this book but to take some action with the content. It is designed to be used and processed, not to merely be flipped through and glanced over. Please do dedicate a journal to have as your companion through your journey here, and feel free to share this with others. These are great topics of conversation with your spouse, your kids, your friends and even for an accountability group, mastermind or book club. There's nothing in here that is earth-shatteringly unique—aside from my targeted effort to lure you into taking action on the book's content as you're reading along. This is about more than maybe thinking about taking some action one day because it seemed like a good idea when you read it in a book once. I want so much more for you than that, and I know from experience that once you start taking a few actions that lead to positive growth and transformation and you experience those results, it will encourage you to do even more! You are on your own path towards being *Blessed and Unstoppable*.

TAKE ACTION: Envision the Best Version of You

1) Journal: Write a description of the version of you that you are working to become. Answer the questions: 1. How does this person treat themselves—how do they eat, exercise, practice self-care, what do they think about themselves, how do they manage stress? 2. How do they manage their money—how to they earn an income, what is their income, how do they spend their money, how do they save and invest their money, how to they budget and plan their finances? 3. What are they like as a person— what is their general mood, how do they treat others: from family to strangers, what are their values and priorities and how do they demonstrate this? 4. What are their dreams, goals and aspirations? 5. What is their lifestyle—where do they live, what car do they drive, what vacations do they take, how do they give back to their community?

2) Visualization: Visualize being that person, at least twice daily for at least 20 minutes. What does it feel like to be that person? How do they start their day? How do they

show their gratitude? Visualize doing the work that they would do, having the relationships that they have, seeing everything that they would see…Be in that moment as that person.

3) Take action: Set goals that will bring you into closer alignment with being that best version of you. List three action items that you can take part in right now to fulfill that alignment and start taking action right now.

CHAPTER 2: Crushing Limiting Beliefs

Defining Your Obstacles to Success

If you're reading this book, the chances are really good that you want something different in life—something bigger, more purposeful, more inspiring. You likely have particular goals or a dream of what your life could be. Maybe you'd like to achieve a greater level of professional success, or maybe it's your personal life where you'd like to experience more passion, commitment and growth. No matter what, if you're reading this book, you're looking to amplify success in at least one, if not more, areas of your life!

It's also safe to say that if you're seeking to level-up success in your life, you've hit some obstacles trying to get there on your own, right? Life keeps getting in your way. Maybe you can't find enough time or the stress from your current situation makes getting to the next level too difficult. Maybe the people in your life are so negative that you always feel beat down every time you talk about your goals and dreams, and you feel defeated before you even take the next step. Perhaps you hear all of these thoughts in your head convincing you that you're just not good enough to grab those dreams, that you'll never have the discipline or resources to achieve what you want, and maybe you feel like you just don't deserve that success you want in the first place...

If any of that rings true for you, then you're reading the right book! I've had all of those same feelings, obstacles and thoughts. Not only did I have them, I was 100% committed to them! Let me tell you where that lead me—I felt trapped in a life that had no future. Thankfully, through years of struggle, I found a way out, and what I want to do is give you the opportunity to learn from my struggle so that you won't have to struggle as hard and as long as I did. This is the short-cut to success!

You see, I was convinced that I was stupid. From the very beginning, there was no one who would be able to tell me otherwise—I even failed kindergarten. Who fails kindergarten? Well, I had to repeat it, and from there I was stuck in a rut of academic failure and special classes. Today, I probably would have been diagnosed with Attention Deficit Hyperactivity Disorder—better known as ADHD. But when I was growing up, they just called you a "slow learner."

Of course, no one ever called me "stupid"—they were too kind to do that—but I watched my siblings and friends really succeed in school, and my grades were so poor, I wasn't even allowed to play sports most of the season. They'd bench you if your grades weren't good enough. It didn't take much for me to decide that I just wasn't smart enough to have success like most of the people around me. I committed to that identity and full of youthful stubbornness, this became an ingrained part of my how I saw myself every day in nearly everything I did in life. I held onto that identity as hard as I could hold onto anything: I was stupid.

This was my core limiting belief, so you'll see me relate back to it often through the chapters. A limiting belief is something that usually takes hold of you when you're younger, and since it's a part of your belief system—as strong as your belief in God or the law of gravity—it's not easy to shake even if it seems irrational or harmful. But, unlike other beliefs, like your belief in God and the law of gravity, your limiting beliefs are uniquely harmful, and they can prevent you from even dreaming and setting goals, and they can certainly prevent you from achieving them.

This is why, as I tell my story throughout this book, you'll often see this particular limiting belief of mine appear. I stayed in a constant battle with this most of my life, and even today, its ghost still likes to appear as a reminder of the harsh struggle I've had with it.

Limiting beliefs don't have to start when you're young though. A traumatic event such as a serious injury or a diagnosis of a terrible illness, an abusive relationship, an addiction, a hostile workplace—there are many instances where a limiting belief can form at any stage of life. The best way to identify your limiting beliefs is to take an inventory of the reasons, or excuses you use, when you don't pursue that goal or dream. What messages do you say to yourself when you tell yourself why you're not doing something or pursuing something you really want?

Identifying Your Limiting Beliefs

When you dig down and get completely honest with yourself, your limiting beliefs will emerge. Often it's really helpful to do this digging with someone you trust, like your spouse, a close friend or a life coach. He or she can help you talk through and can even be instrumental in providing helpful insights into what your particular limiting beliefs are. You have to identify it before you can change it, so this is the starting point.

You might also notice a couple of things as you do this work:

1) You'll see how a limiting belief might get triggered unexpectedly in your life. For instance, if you were overweight growing up, maybe you were teased about it, you were certainly self-conscious about it, then in your relationship with your partner, he or she mentions something about your body that sends you on a spiral of emotions—a

spiral that doesn't really align with the spirit of the comment, but you're in this dark place in your head anyway.

2) You might over compensate for your limiting belief in some other area of your life. For instance, if you're lacking confidence over your particular limiting belief, we still crave a sense of confidence, so often you'll find confidence in another area of your life, maybe a little disproportionately, because you're making up for your insecurities surrounding your limiting belief.

For example, when I was in the eighth grade, I remember that girls started to notice me. So, okay, I was convinced that I was stupid, but girls think I'm really good-looking. I specifically remember that there was this beautiful Asian girl that I really, really had a crush on, and I found out that she liked me, too. The guys didn't think much of me—I could never stick with sports because my grades were so poor, but the girls thought I was hot.

The sadness of being not-so-smart, and fighting these feelings of worthlessness every day, and struggling with homework, not being able to understand it, and taking two or three hours to complete something that a normal kid would get done in an hour—it was crushing. But the girls, they didn't care about my grades. They thought I was good-looking, and that gave me a sense of confidence that I gripped onto and used to compensate for feeling so worthless otherwise.

This carried into high school, and I really cashed in on it into adulthood as an exotic dancer—I even posed in an issue of Playgirl Magazine!

Still, that limiting belief plagued me every day of my life: I'm stupid, so I better use my looks because I don't have any brains to help get me through life.

In school, the pain and insecurity didn't end just because I found a different source of confidence. I was a year behind everyone else, and I was in Slow Learning Disability (SLD) classes, and the kids of course noticed that I wasn't in the same classes with them at school. I put up a shield, making fun of it before they could, taking their ammunition away, and we'd all laugh about it together. Believe me, it still stung, but I learned how to protect myself from it being torture.

Vulnerability and Breaking Down Walls

We develop walls and shields to protect us from the pain our limiting beliefs cause all the time, and when we let those walls and shields down, allow ourselves to become raw and vulnerable, that's precisely the place where change can happen. Most people, however, are content to leave those protective barriers in-place at all times, guarding their limiting beliefs from scrutiny or even self-examination. It hurts; it's a little scary to go beyond those walls. We're unsure how we'll handle it or what will happen, so we keep it all closed off. In doing so, we prevent ourselves from ever fully healing; we don't feel the power of releasing these toxic beliefs that don't serve us and our goals and that likely aren't even true.

My limiting belief of feeling stupid lead me down a particular path in life. I dropped out of high school, and surprisingly my dad let me do it without too much of a fight, but there was a hard rule: I could leave high school as long as I got a job. I really was surprised that he let me drop out, but now I had to find a job without even having a high school diploma, GED

30

or even being enrolled in school of any kind. Here I am filling out job applications, and I have to put down when I graduated from high school. Good friends were helping me get interviews, but as soon as they found out that I didn't even have a GED, that was the end for every opportunity beyond earning minimum wage.

Time after time this would happen, and with people who knew me, and I felt beat down. I was a loser, a straight-up loser. This limiting belief was being reinforced literally everywhere I went. It ate at me. And then someone would say, "Well, why don't you just go get your GED"?

Okay, so I'm going to do this—I'm going to earn my GED. I studied for three months in an adult program, and I was ready for the test. The teachers knew I was ready for the test; we had been working on this for months for hours, three times a week, and I felt completely prepared. I was so excited! But the test was timed. My stomach flew up to my throat—I don't pass anything that's timed. I'm slow; I'm stupid; I can't do this. My limiting beliefs took over, and I started obsessing over: I'm never going to pass this test!

When I sat down for the test, feeling absolutely ready but still freaked out about it being timed, I tried to focus. But I kept looking at the clock. I was trying not to with everything in me, but I kept looking up and looking up. I was thinking: *I shouldn't even be sitting here. Why am I doing this?* These thoughts popped up about 180 times throughout the test. My limiting beliefs had taken over!

And when I was halfway through the test, I was convinced that there was no way I was not going to make it in time. So, instead of following through because I was so frustrated and

31

so stressed out, feeling absolutely crazy, I Christmas-tree'd the other half of the test—just marking in random answers.

I didn't pass. Feeling completely defeated, I convinced myself to do it again. It took all of my courage to sit back down in that room and take that test again, still feeling prepared but still feeling panicked by the time, the exact same scenario repeated. But this time, would you believe that when I got my score back, I still failed? But I failed by just one point. I gave up. I'm stupid and slow, and I just can't get my GED. Getting a good job now is not going to happen.

My head was racing… by failing by one point, it didn't get me excited; I was so frustrated. Okay, you know what? This is my second time. I couldn't finish this the first time. I couldn't finish the second time. I failed it by Christmas tree in the second half by one point. I could have had my graduation papers with just one more point. That just made my head spin. So, you know what? I'm stupid—I'm not meant to graduate. That's it. I'm not putting myself through this again!

One point off, fear of going through that for another round and potentially experiencing that exact failure one more time, it was too much. I dug into my limiting beliefs at that point— I kept giving up. Everything took too long for me to do, and I'd never be good enough. But, today, of course I know that this isn't true. It might take me a little longer to read a book than it does for many people, but I love to read books now!

You see, the limiting belief is not that I have a learning disability—that part is fact. The limiting belief was that I was stupid, unable to learn, and that I didn't deserve to be successful with anything that required me to be smart. That limiting belief was absolutely false!

Our Weaknesses Can Be Strengths

In time, I learned better how I processed information, that I could read a book slowly, one chapter at a time. I crushed my limiting beliefs by being vulnerable enough to accept the part that's fact and developing ways to do what works best for me. I'm not stupid at all—I've destroyed that limiting belief for myself. I manage a business, I help others, and I've launched my own business. Oh, and look—I've written a book!

I've also learned that there's a lot of value to reading a chapter at a time for everyone, versus speeding through a book in a few days. Because when you read a chapter a day, you get to absorb it and assimilate that information. Think about how you might read personal development books like this one—if you speed through it, are you really absorbing the information to the best of your ability? Are you applying the information you read in your head, and are you brainstorming along with the content in the chapter? Are you journaling to really delve into the lessons provided?

Maybe slowing down the reading process a little, only focusing on one chapter a day, would be beneficial to more people, not just me. Plus, maybe that strategy is beneficial to other areas in our lives where taking our time to fully absorb the information about it could help us make better, more thoughtful and even more intuitive decisions, more in-line with our true intentions and goals.

Confronting Your Limiting Beliefs

There's an activity that I recommend people do to begin identifying and confronting their own limiting beliefs. Either

33

in your journal, on a sheet of paper, your computer, or your phone—I have a lot of notes I keep on my phone—start writing. Every time you feel anything less than, any time you feel frightened to move forward, any time you give an excuse for not doing something that will benefit you or for doing something that will hurt you, usually a limiting belief is behind it. Find it and write it down.

Often your best friend or your spouse is going to know what many of your limiting beliefs are, too. They've watched you struggle and make excuses, and they can likely point these out to you, hopefully in a nice kind of way.

The next step is to review these notes at the end of each day and focus on changing your mindset and changing those beliefs in these areas. The more frequently you do this, you'll begin to develop the habit, and you'll start to catch yourself before the limiting belief gets a chance to drive your actions. You'll then be in greater control of your own thoughts and destiny to turn your thinking around and arm yourself with a renewed power-driven mindset.

There is a direct link between your limiting beliefs and what is holding you back from achieving your goals and dreams. Success isn't something that just happens by chance; it's not an accident. It takes people many years and tireless trial and error to become an "overnight success". Identifying, confronting and replacing your limiting beliefs are critical to achieving the success you want. If you're looking for shortcuts, *this is the shortcut!*

One important connection to make is the link between your limiting beliefs and how you actually define who you are. Oh, sure, I might not have outwardly described myself to others as being stupid, but that is absolutely how I defined myself. It became a fact of who I was as a person, and it limited me from even trying or believing in myself to do anything that required some brains. When in fact, I am not stupid at all, and that is no longer a part of my identity. I do still learn differently from others, so I've made adjustments to learn the way that works best for me. This shift in thinking—in abandoning my limiting belief to one that is empowering—has enabled me to set goals, achieve things that I never thought were possible, and build upon success after success in my life.

I shifted my mindset from "I can't" to "I'll try" to "I must", and that lead to success. That all stemmed from abandoning my limiting belief. I'd still be stuck in the same miserable place I was in if it weren't for doing the hard work of confronting what I most feared—myself.

When your mindset is stuck in your limiting beliefs you truly think you think that your limiting beliefs are who you are. It's not just a matter of what you think; you actually become a certain way because of your limiting beliefs. So, the opposite is also true. By shifting your mindset, you can actually become someone different when you start taking the steps to take the power away from your limiting beliefs. When you can start saying to yourself: *I realize that this is not who I am. This is the limits of beliefs that I've brought onto myself.*

We've been told that a man is what he thinks, so your limiting beliefs, because they are false by nature, have not allowed you to be your most authentic self. And this is why I think I've become and you've become some made-up character based on your false beliefs, and those beliefs have prevented you from being your most powerful, authentic self.

Same example: You can become a character of someone different once you start shifting your mindset, believing in things that are true about yourself, changing your words, changing the people you hang out with—your circle of influence and completely changing your focus, conversations and actions. You get to be the person you've dreamed of becoming.

Change Your Words = Change Your Life

More often than we realize, our language dictates how we feel and how we respond to things. We often think of words as being an expression of how we feel and how we respond, but I'm inviting you to flip this thinking around to put you in more control of shaping who you are. Word choices are a profound indicator of our limiting beliefs, so when we deliberately shift them, we purposefully disempower our limiting beliefs. Think about it this way: if you have a limiting belief that money is scarce, and you can't afford the things that you need, let alone the things that you want, you probably often use phrases like: "I can't afford that" or "that's too expensive" or "I'll never be able to afford to do that". What if you commit to never saying those phrases again, but instead you replaced those phrases with: "let me find a way to pay for that" or "how can I build the resources to afford that" or "I'll be able to afford that in two years if I follow this plan"?

When you do this, you allow your word choices to shape your mindset versus allowing your false beliefs to control your words.

I can say for a fact that changing my words has changed my life. It's very, very, very emotional for me because too often we live on this autopilot, mindlessly sinking into whatever habits we've accumulated without even realizing it and without considering the consequences of it. The words we use are a huge component in this.

Most of us can relate to friends who use curse words often, and you'll ask them to please not use those words around your children or out in public, and they don't even realize they say those words that often. They're so used to saying those words; they don't intend to be offensive, but it is reflective of their state of mind, and it impacts others around them. They are completely unaware. That's usually true of all of our word choices.

Well, why can't we be so used to saying something else by changing the habits of our word choices? Think about who the person is that you want to be and what words and phrases that person uses and absolutely doesn't use. Your words will not only begin to shape your thoughts and mindset in a different way, but others around you will perceive you differently too! If your words are more decisive, people will see you as a stronger leader. If your words are kinder, people will see you as someone they can trust. If your words are more positive, people will see you as someone they look forward to hearing.

Take a moment and think about the person you want to become. For myself, I thought about who is the person I want to be ten years from now? What words and phrases would he be speaking? How will others feel around him? How will he feel about himself when he speaks? I really, really want to be in it: a walking, living example, so I need to make these changes today. If I wait ten years and expect this new person to magically emerge on his own, I'll be another 10

years behind my goal. So, changing my words changed my
life.

TAKE ACTION: Break Through Limiting Beliefs

So now that you've identified your limiting beliefs, and you've
shifted some key word choices and phrases around to use
your words to help reframe your mindset, let's explore
specific steps that you can take to break-through your limiting
beliefs:

1) Journal: Continue documenting moments when
   limiting beliefs are challenging your ability to be your
   most authentic self and are standing in the way of you
   achieving your dreams

2) Journal: At the end of the day for at least the next
   three days, or longer, review your documented
   limiting beliefs and list five actions that you can take
   to overwrite your limiting beliefs. These might
   include: 1. Meditation or prayer to focus on new,
   more empowering beliefs; 2. Interrupting a limiting
   belief that you've identified when it comes to mind
   and replace it with a new, more empowering core
   belief; 3. Take part in a physical activity such as
   walking or running, swimming, cycling, etc. and focus
   your mind on more empowering beliefs to replace
   your limiting beliefs; 4. Take part in a creative activity
   such as writing, drawing, dancing, sculpting and focus
   on your new empowering beliefs; 5. Talk with a
   trusted partner, mentor, coach or friend about the
   limiting beliefs you've identified and what you would
   like to replace them with—discuss with this person

methods to hold yourself accountable to develop this new mindset.

CHAPTER 3: Mindset Mastery

As I mentioned previously, from as far back as I can remember, I always believed I was stupid, and I want to dive into this story a little deeper because it truly is the core to my personal limiting belief. Diving into the core of your biggest limiting belief will become an immense healing process for you, too. This massive devaluing of myself has been the biggest struggle of my life. It has plagued me and understanding the specific genesis of it was critical for me to be able to finally overcome it. Understanding it more completely through the wisdom of hindsight has allowed me to pull the plug on its power over me, and that's huge!

Yet to this day, there's still a bit of it that haunts me, that ignites a struggle, so you'll see it mentioned throughout these chapters here and there. And where it all began, this decision that I was stupid, wasn't at home, not directly or intentionally, anyway. My parents were great and never insulted me. My conclusion was derived through a sordid succession of evidence that I compiled in my mind. It began as a very young child, and the evidence kept building for me well into adulthood.

Looking back, I can deconstruct the evidence more clearly than when I was living it, and that perspective let's me better define exactly what happened. In fact, I wasn't stupid at all. I have a learning disability that we now know how to identify and treat better in the 21st Century than we did in the 20th Century. I just needed a little more time than others and to break lessons into smaller pieces, but I couldn't figure that out until I was brave enough to go back in time and dissect it, reinvestigate it for myself.

It all started when I failed kindergarten. Who fails kindergarten? And then, all through middle school and high school, I was in SLD classes. That stands for: Slow Learning

42

Disability. To me, SLD stood for: Stupid, Less than, Degenerate. So, what does someone do that feels Stupid, Less than, Degenerate? It's not some deeply-held mystery—we usually drop out of school. This led to more and more self-destructive behaviors and incredibly self-defeating thoughts that I held onto as gospel. My belief that I was stupid carried with me through most of my life, and it was the lens through which I viewed everything. I was as convinced of this truth about myself as much as I believed I needed oxygen to breathe.

When you believe you aren't worth much, you don't do much of anything with any great success. It is a really solid self-fulfilling prophecy. Failed work history, failed businesses, and five failed marriages served to support my conclusion about myself—I was worthless. Seriously, prove me wrong!

No matter what, though, I always kept a spark of faith in God, and I attended church regularly. I might be stupid, but I always knew that there was something greater than me guiding me, allowing me to have hope and maybe the slightest sense of purpose. Then one day in church, when I was feeling particularly low, wallowing in my many failures, I heard the preacher talk about the twelve disciples that Jesus would pick to walk the lands and spread the Gospel. This story wasn't new to me, of course, but on this day, I heard it in a new way—in a way that spoke to my heart. The preacher explained that Jesus picked very broken men to be his disciples. He didn't choose the best of the best. He hung out with people who were outcasts; people like me. Just then, a little light of hope sparked in my spirit—a light that wasn't there a moment ago. I thought, if Jesus chose these guys to hang out with, well I'm not so bad after all. Some of the things these disciples have done were a lot worse than

43

anything I've done. Maybe I'm okay—maybe I'm incredible--in comparison.

That little light in my spirit began to grow, and this amazing idea popped into my head: God can use a broken man, someone like me, to change the world, just as he led His disciples! That's when hope was really born for me. Then and there, I decided to no longer allow my past to control my future, and I opened my heart to becoming someone different—*Blessed and Unstoppable*!

The road hasn't been easy. Nothing worthwhile ever is, and it's a daily commitment to always becoming the best version of me that I can be for you. That's right, for you! Because if I get the privilege of reaching you in some way at all, even if it's just through this book, then everything I've done and gone through is a blessing, and I am forever grateful.

The first step to becoming the new me was rough because I had to challenge these deep-seeded thoughts that I held about myself for all of my life: Stupid, Less than, Degenerate. To become this new person, *Blessed and Unstoppable*, I must re-set my mindset each day, every single day, to continue becoming the best version of me for you.

In this chapter, I'm going to give you the exact blueprint that I've used to help me shift my mindset daily, and it's the same strategy I use to coach my clients—it's the foundation to purpose-driven and lasting transformation.

Re-set Button for Your Day

What would it mean to you if you could push a reset button on your day? Maybe the day before was rough—you might be fighting with your wife or husband, your kids are mad at you for something, your boss just assigned a pile of work to you along with a deadline that feels impossible, and to top it all off, you got some really bad news you need to deal with. You managed the day the best you could, and you finally made it to bed exhausted and feeling beat up. We've all had these days. But what if I told you, that you could just push a button so that in the morning, every morning, you could wake up feeling brand new, optimistic, clear-headed, powerful, blessed and unstoppable? It's true; you can. You have the ability to do this each and every day of your life if you want it. But you have to want it, then you have to do the work to get it.

Developing this skill of resetting your mindset for each day is one of the most powerful things you could ever do for yourself. It allows you to look at any adversity or challenge you're facing objectively to see the positive in difficult times and to get creative with solutions that might seem insurmountable when you're stuck in the emotions and negative self-talk that usually drives us under harsh conditions.

In fact, there are specific steps that you can take and turn into healthy, positive habits to ensure that each and every day comes with this reset button, and it begins with preparing for it the night before.

Step 1: Journaling. I know, not everyone is comfortable writing anything down, but I promise that it's a highly effective tool to get the thoughts out of your head and in a space where it's easier to take action on them and resolve

45

them. Plus, I have a few tips to make it a little easier for you. First, get honest with yourself about all of the stuff you're dealing with, and just list them on the page. Ignoring problems, minimizing them or just blowing up about them only feeds them so that they become bigger problems. Naming the problems actually reduces their power in your head, and you can see them from a different perspective— something you can take action on versus just something that's haunting you.

Second, next to each problem write down your dream resolution. It might be something as simple as a weight loss goal, or it might be something much scarier like surviving cancer. Whatever it is, envision that problem resolved and describe what that looks like. Third, write just a few reasonable steps you can take within the next day or the next week to help resolve the problems you've listed. Understanding, of course, that these steps may not solve your problems completely, but you'll gain some power over them just by committing to taking some action towards resolving them. These actions may be as simple as conducting some research, having a tough conversation, signing up with a personal trainer or asking for help with something that's been difficult for you. The key here is to make these actions really doable and taking small steps towards resolving the things weighing on you.

This one activity, journaling like this, will help you purge your negative mindset so that you can have a more peaceful night and a clear mind as you go to sleep because you have actively addressed everything you're worrying about. Most things can't be solved in a day or a week, but you know that taking the first few steps towards resolution is how everything eventually gets achieved, and you're now on your way.

Step 2: Good Night's Sleep. Have you heard of the phrase "sleep hygiene"? If you Google it, you might be amazed by the amount of resources available on the subject. That's not surprising since American adults are literally plagued with insomnia. A huge part of the reason why you've already effectively addressed if you've begun your journaling assignment in Step 1—purge your anxiety over not addressing the problems that are causing you stress!

The next effective step you need to take is to develop an action plan for getting a good night's sleep. Begin by examining how many hours you actually tend to sleep per night. If you're not sure about your sleeping patterns—maybe you wake up in the middle of the night, have a hard time getting back to sleep or maybe you don't really remember—there are apps and devices, some as simple as a Fitbit, that can help you track your sleep patterns to get an honest assessment on how great you're really sleeping each night.

Examine this with absolute honesty and then think about how this might be affecting your day. Do you maintain your energy levels throughout the day, or do you experience a mid-day slump (note that more than poor sleeping habits could be contributing to this such as nutrition, etc.)? Do you have difficulty waking up each morning feeling refreshed and ready to begin your morning routine? Are you especially irritable in the mornings or throughout the day—not getting enough sleep can really impact your mood? What about your memory, ability to focus, ability to manage daily stress? Yes, not having adequate sleep can cause issues with all of these.

So let's examine your sleep hygiene. As I mentioned, it's a good idea to Google this for real in-depth specifics, but some key points to note aside from journaling the night before include:

47

- **Electronics:** Turning off all electronics and possibly removing them from your bedroom before you go to sleep and using only a simple alarm to help you wake up in the morning. There is a lot of science behind this, but the short version of why this is important is that these serve as distractions to keep you awake: from email and social media notifications to television and even the pesky lights on your devices as they charge up or cast dull light in your room. Definitely shutting off these devices or removing them from your room entirely can really help assist with sleep.

- **Room temperature:** Be aware of how comfortable the temperature in the room is for you when you sleep. For many people, the specific temperature differs when they define comfort—to some it's 68-70 degrees, others need it around 75-78 degrees, and everything in between. This can get really tricky as most adults tend to sleep with another person, so you might want to actually have a conversation about this. Maybe consider adding another blanket to keep the person who gets cold easily comfortable, or the one who gets warm easily might need just a light sheet and wear lighter clothing to bed. In general, most people sleep better in a cool, completely dark room.

- **Alcohol and meals:** Avoid alcohol and heavy meals just before bed. That might seem counter-intuitive, but there's real science behind this, too. Alcohol dehydrates you, quickly and severely. While it might make you feel sleepy, it actually tends to prevent sound sleep and also tends to lead to interrupting sleep with indigestion, urination, headaches and other issues. This is the same for heavy meals. A light snack and a few sips of water are usually perfectly fine just before bed.

- **Hydration:** While drinking lots of fluids right before bed is not a great idea because you'll either have to urinate in the middle of the night or wake up with an uncomfortable, overly full bladder, making sure that you're properly hydrated throughout the day is critical. There are charts available online to help you determine the healthiest amount of water intake for your weight and size, but at minimum, everyone should drink at least eight glasses of water per day (about 8 oz of water per glass). Honestly, more is better, but cut out the fluids about an hour before you go to bed to allow your bladder to empty, and just have a few sips to keep you comfortable. Dehydration can lead to sleep disturbances, headaches, dry mouth, cramps, etc., so keep the water flowing throughout the day.

- **Prepare for sleep:** It's really important to develop healthy before-bed habits that can include taking a hot shower or bath to relax you, and it actually brings down your body when you exit the hot water temperature to help you sleep. Making sure your bedroom is decluttered, clean sheets and a made bed—all will help you relax and fall and stay asleep longer. A soothing cup of herbal tea and/or a light, healthy snack an hour before bed can help satiate you through the night and curb any midnight cravings. Reading an inspirational book or anything you really enjoy or listening to music that reduces stress and relaxes you can also be a great part of your before-bed routine.

These are just of a few key tips among many to help you overcome sleeplessness and insomnia because not getting a proper amount of solid sleep will interfere with nearly all areas of your life and hinder you reaching optimum health and success. Your mood, focus, energy, stamina, memory, stress management, creativity and even your internal drive and motivation can all be severely undermined if you're not beginning each day well-rested and re-charged.

Now that you've had a great night's sleep, the next thing you need to do is to commit to waking up in a positive mindset. So far, you've purged your problems and set action items to each, so they are now in the process of being solved. You literally no longer have to "worry" and stress about them—just take the actions you've already committed to taking. Then, you made sure you slept well, and in the process, you're also well-hydrated—all of this will help address morning sluggishness and feelings of dread.

Step 3: Morning Mindset. Let's discuss gratitude—I know, people talk about this all of the time. Maybe you're not convinced that this really will make a huge difference in your life, but I assure you that this is a critical step in effectively pushing that reset button on your day. Begin your day with a positive mindset, and that begins with gratitude.

If you can take your own pulse, and you happen to have you, you have every reason to be grateful. A bunch of people did not wake up this morning, and they never will again. The fact that you did, you've achieved the most important thing you can do today. Your family, friends, the people who count on you, love you and enjoy you, all still have you here on this planet, and that's awesome!

No matter your circumstances, even if you feel alone, frightened, abandoned, hopeless—you have this day to create something new, better, inspired and loving. Embrace it! Even if you have to force a smile—smile. Find something to laugh about. Find something to celebrate—even if it's small, like you actually found matching socks this morning. Choose to be grateful for your life and the small things around you every morning, and you'll push that reset button.

Sometimes when life gets to be the darkest, stress builds up and fear starts to take hold, we forget that there are little actions we can take every step of the way to empower us, to give us joy, to allow us to take charge and decide to be a different, better, stronger, healthier, more loving and positive version of ourselves each day. Well, it's absolutely true!

What are you grateful for right now? Think of 20 things right now that you're grateful for—it doesn't matter how silly or small or large and imaginative the things are on your list. Just list them, and don't cheat yourself—you must list a full 20. If this exercise seems hard to do, it's that much more important for you to make the effort to do it.

Step 4: Make your bed. Ask your average teenager why it's important to make your bed, and you'll often hear a response like: "It's stupid, because you're just going to unmake it again in a few hours." Or they might say, "It's just a bed, who cares?" You know, they're not entirely wrong, but there's a bigger picture here—a deeper reason why the simple act of making your bed each morning is a really effective part of pushing that reset button on your day.

According to the 2014 commencement address at the University of Texas at Austin by Admiral William H McRaven, he said that when you wake up and make your bed each morning,

51

you've completed your first task for the day which leads to many other tasks being completed. It builds a momentum of accomplishments, and it reminds you to pay attention to the details because they always matter. How you do one thing is how you do everything. Then if at the end of the day, you've had a difficult day, you come home to a bed that you made, reminding you that you can have a better day tomorrow.

Step 5: Workout. It's really difficult to be at your best in your professional or personal relationships if your energy is low, your stress levels are high or if you feel out-of-shape and less than your best in your physical and mental health. One of the most effective ways to reset your physical and mental health is through physical fitness. For most people, the link between being physically fit and their physical health seems obvious—your heart, bones, muscles and other vital organs all perform better when your weight management is under control and you're using your body to build strength and resilience. What some people may not understand is the extreme benefits physical fitness and exercise has on mental health.

Let me be perfectly clear—I'm not saying that exercise is in any way a substitution for physician or psychiatric care, physician prescribed medication or therapeutic treatment for any diagnosed ailment—physically or mentally. What I am saying is that also combining physical fitness and exercise can have enormous positive benefits in all areas of your life. You only have one body, and the proper care of that body includes keeping it in shape to the best of our ability. There is science to support the fact that regular exercise is highly effective in addressing not only weight management and physical health but also can have positive results in managing stress, depression, anxiety, focus, energy, memory, mood, creativity and overall mental clarity.

Step 6: Eat nutritious food. I could write a whole book on healthy diets and nutrition for optimum health and performance, and maybe I'll publish one as a companion to this book at some point, but for right now, let's just cover a few basics that aren't difficult to implement in our fast-paced, too-often fast junk food culture. The most basic thing there is to say is that if you are really committed to hitting the restart button on your day, pay attention to how you fuel your body. Food is medicine, right? If you put a whole lot of junk into you—sugar, chemicals, large amounts of fat and processed carbohydrates—you will stress out your body by feeding it high calorie, low nutrient foods.

Much like proper physical fitness, poor nutrition can also lead to inconsistent energy levels, along with extreme highs and huge drops. It can cause issues with focus, performance, and increase your chances of getting ill, impacting your immune system causing increased stress and difficulty managing daily stress.

On the other hand, by focusing on eating an all-natural, healthful diet, you can super-charge your long-term energy flow throughout the day, increase focus and resiliency, and it will help you achieve peak performance in all areas of your life as you're properly fueling your body with the nutrients it needs and not burdening it with a bunch of empty calories and harmful chemicals that it doesn't need to process. There are many different kinds of healthy meal plans out there that you can find through a Google search which you can follow. My only advice right now has to do with finding something that isn't too extreme, something that seems like a realistic healthful solution for you, and one that begins with a healthy breakfast to start your day on-track.

Step 7: Set a daily agenda. First, begin with the things you know you must accomplish for the day: family responsibilities, work responsibilities, etc. Get all of those set into your agenda along with the actions you need to take, scheduling, follow-up, etc. Then, re-visit your journal activity from the night before when you listed all of your problems and the actions you intend to take today or this week to help resolve them and add them into your agenda. Some of these might be very uncomfortable and hard, but prioritize them, and take those steps you need to take to accomplish them. When you start crossing these items in particular off of your list because you've completed them, you'll likely feel that weight on your shoulders lift even more.

Strategies for Mindset Shifting

Now that you've achieved pushing that re-set button on your day, which is an activity you'll want to continue and fine-tune every day as these positive habits form and start to shape and transform your life? You're ready to move on to your next step of your *Blessed and Unstoppable* life plan! This isn't a rulebook, but it is a roadmap. Like any map there are side streets, highways, scenic routes, detours and obstacles. There isn't just one way to do anything, and not everything works for all people all of the time in all situations. What this section is aiming to do is to provide you with "Strategies for mindset shifting" that have worked for me and have been wildly successful for many others that may allow you to take a shortcut. This shortcut involves helping you to avoiding some of those most common obstacles and detours that many people before you and I have endured and learned their way around. When we share information like these tips, the goal is to get you to fast-forward through the tough experiences and life lessons many of us endured the hard way, through

54

experience and trial and error, that allowed us to arrive at success.

Strategies for mindset shifting involve:

- **Prioritize personal development:** Research the experts who have achieved what you're seeking to achieve and model after them. I'm not suggesting that you try to become the next Tony Robbins, Les Brown or Dave Ramsey—although you could be—but instead to look at your heroes and study their paths to the success you'd like to achieve. Most of them have videos, books, courses, Social media groups, masterminds and coaching opportunities that will allow you to learn from the very best in the strategies you'd like to master.

- **Invest in yourself and your goals:** There's a difference between spending money, time and energy and investing in these things. Understanding this distinction is incredibly important when you're strategizing your mindset shift. When I spend money, it's gone. I usually exchange it for something of value, but ultimately, I'm not going to see that money ever again, and whatever I spent that money on is going to be near worthless or greatly depreciate in value and soon as I purchase it. The same is true for time and energy spent. However, when I invest my money, I anticipate getting out MORE than what I invested. There's always some risk, but if you invest intelligently, and I suspect that you do because you're taking the time and effort to read a book on this, the rewards quickly outweigh the risks. So, research those classes, that mentor, the opportunity before you, and

55

invest wisely in yourself and your goals for your future.

- **Enroll in coaching:** Olympic and pro athletes all have coaches, and most often those coaches are not and have never been as successful as participants in the sports they are coaching as the superstars they coach. So why do these athletes who are far superior in skill and talent than the people coaching them bother with even having a coach? Because that's how you become your best! Nobody is actually capable of seeing themselves objectively, and self-motivation, self-accountability and advising one's self isn't nearly as effective as someone who is gifted at being that expert for someone else. I highly recommend interviewing and enrolling a coach to work with you on achieving your goals, and with the right fit, you'll watch your performance skyrocket!

- **3 positive changes:** Retrain your brain by noticing and rewarding three positive changes per day. That's right! You're on the critical path towards creating positive habits and retraining your brain to an elevated, success-driven mindset, and the most effective way to get these good habits to take hold and rewire your brain for success is to pay close attention to the changes you make as they happen. Have you improved your diet and fitness? Acknowledge it and reward yourself. Have you improved your sleep habits? Take note and reward it. Have you been journaling and setting your daily agendas? Notice this and give yourself a gift: a couple hours doing something you really love, a small purchase of something you enjoy. Just something to pat yourself on the back and make you smile to reinforce your achievements.

TAKE ACTION: Mindset Mastery

This whole chapter is aligned with taking action specifically to shift your mindset to become the best version of you. I encourage you to visit each part of this chapter with your journal and map out how you will take action on each element described above.

Other tools that will be very helpful in taking action on this chapter include using a calendar to schedule action items you intend to implement at specific times of the day and setting alarm alerts on your phone. Creating good habits is all about developing a sense of discipline and adherence to routine— usually out of the normal for most people. Let that last line sink in for a second, "Usually out of the norm for most people."

That's right—most people live their lives in a state of reacting to everything around them, somewhat mindlessly. When you approach life each morning with deliberate mindfulness, discipline for positivity and routine to create a better you— that's when you step out and become different from the masses. The work you put into developing your elevated mindset is exactly what gets you on the path towards getting everything you want in life.

To achieve an exceptional life, it requires you to do things that most people never think to do. It's all about putting in the work, creating those great habits then change is unavoidable.

CHAPTER 4: The Power of Words

Viewing Challenges

When you start off in life absolutely convinced that you are "below-average", everything is stacked against you. When you look at a challenge through that lens, you're already defeated. You're certain you'll fail. Everyone else will do it better than you. It's not even worth trying, and so you sabotage any potential you might have for success completely in your mind then you follow that through with your actions to ensure your dialogue is consistent with the outcome. You literally fail before you even try.

The seed of this for me was, again, planted as early as kindergarten, as I'm just starting to develop any sense of self-awareness and socialize with other kids seeing how I might measure up—just wishing to be "normal" or "average", but I'm told that I have to be held back, and that everybody I knew from my first year in school is going to go forward. Everyone, except me, and I have to stay back with kids younger than me, kids I don't know. I know I'm there with them because I'm not smart enough to be with the kids my own age, so I never believed I'd be able to take on any challenges. Stupid kids don't succeed, right?

I'm literally learning who I am through this lens, becoming who I am and developing my first sense of an identity as a kid who isn't good enough, who is stupid, who can't succeed. That was the foundation for my mindset. This was reinforced through elementary school as I was still slower than the rest of these kids who were younger than me. So by the time I entered middle school and high school, and I was put into in SLD classes, I never even got to feel like I was average; I never even developed an average mindset. When you're in special classes for special people, that's a kind of "special" that doesn't feel good. I started my life being ashamed of who I was.

To add insult to injury, growing up with my brother and my sister, of course, they were mostly A students, above average all the way. And I'd wonder why I was the stupid one; what's wrong with me? It made everything even harder for me, because my brother and my sister excelled in school, and I was so obviously the dumb one in the family, and I formulated a way of thinking based on my experience with all of this. Words in my head berated me: slow, stupid, less than, degenerate, loser, failure, embarrassment, unworthy, rejected…

As I grew older, though, I noticed that I had a couple of positive traits. I was okay at sports, for instance. Of course, that still crushed me because to play sports in school, you had to keep up a certain grade point average to stay on a team. I'd try so hard to keep my grades up, because I wanted to play sports so badly. At the beginning of each year, I'd try out and start with a sport, but by the time grades were posted, I was eventually benched, then kicked off the team.

The other positive trait I discovered about myself is that girls thought I was really good looking. I loved that attention! However, the grades became a problem with that, too because in my family the rules were that if our grades slipped to Cs and Ds, which really one impacted me, we weren't allowed to go to skating parties and hang out with friends after school, so my social life wasn't great no matter how much positive attention I was getting from the girls.

I would even hide my report card when I knew I wanted to do something, and I'd be grounded for getting a D in a class. One time, when I heard there was a skating party, I was supposed to meet this girl there. I had such a crush on her, and she was going to be at the skating party. I knew our

61

report cards were coming out the same day, and I definitely had a D which meant there was no way my parents were going to let me go skating. So I told my parents that the report cards never came; they were coming out Monday. Well, of course my mom got a phone call that day from the school, and they advised her that the report cards had been sent home, and they also told her what my grades were.

Then I was grounded for not only one week but for two weeks—first for lying about the report card and second for getting a D.

The reality is that as hard as I would try, the words I had for myself in my head ensured that I would absolutely never succeed. Today I understand very clearly that I am not stupid—I just learn a little differently than most, and it might take me a little more time to focus and process information, but I'm far from stupid. I can and have learned just about everything I've put my mind to, but it took more work for me to change the words I use for myself and for the challenges facing me. It took more work to shift my mindset than any challenge I ever had actually learning anything.

When I felt stupid and less than, challenges were met by trying to lie through them or cover them up versus succeeding. My only weapon to survive was to attempt to deceive people through my failure when I was just trying to do average things and be like average people. I never knew why everything was always stacked against me, but I was always convinced that the problem was that I was somehow defective.

Of course, not everyone had this extreme disadvantage, but also many have had it much worse in different ways. The point is that whatever defenses we used in our past to try to

62

survive through many different kinds of challenges, many of those defenses aren't serving us, but we're still using them because it's what we know; it's what we've relied on our whole lives to get us through. The words we choose to frame our thoughts: I'm not good enough; I'll never be able to afford that; It doesn't matter—I don't need it; I don't deserve happiness; Love never lasts; Everyone is out for themselves; No one cares about me; Everyone lies; I'm not worth it; I give up... these are the nutrients we're feeding our hopes, dreams, aspirations, ambitions and determination.

Challenges Through a Lens of Success

Successful people tend to literally use different words when faced with challenges than people who are less successful on some level. They approach challenges from a place of empowerment, and the words that fire off in their heads before they even take the first action step are more often than not what catapults them to achieve what might seem terribly difficult or even impossible to others.

When your mindset is trained to look for solutions to problems, it's going to find solutions all over the place. However, if your mind is trained to just see reasons why something can't be done, that mind is going to see more barriers than solutions. Shifting your words, how you frame everything, will actually shift what you see and what you're able to achieve.

Feed your mind with better words and literally everything in your world will shift into limitless possibilities. Breaking free from those old words isn't always easy—just because something causes you pain, like toxic self-talk, doesn't mean that it hasn't become extremely comfortable. We find our

63

greatest comfort in what's familiar to us, and often that includes things that are very painful.

To help you shift your words into a consistently positive frame, it requires focus, dedication and deciding that you must make this change right now, no excuses and no exceptions. It requires you to commit to making this change anew each morning and throughout the day until your brain rewires and this new language becomes your new normal.

Fill your world with motivating and uplifting messages, from music and books to watching speakers and likely even changing your circle of friends to ensure that you're being fed positivity all around you. Imagine if your words shift from the negative or the defeated to I am enough; I'm loving and deserve love; I can succeed; I'm valuable; I'll find a way; I can achieve this; I feel supported and loved; I'm excited to have this new challenge; I got this!

I also can't over-state how important and beneficial it is to have a mentor, a coach, to have someone around you that has succeeded in accomplishing something that you want to accomplish. Someone that has the mindset that you want, who can support you in becoming that person you dream of becoming. It's critical to surround yourself with like-minded people or with people who have a mindset that you aspire to have. The more your circle of influence models what you aspire to be, you'll find it much easier to start changing your words, which leads to changing your actions, and soon you'll start becoming that person of your dreams.

It's a process, and it's a long-term commitment to make big transformations. It's not something you can achieve overnight, and it's worth investing in others who can support you on the path—they'll be able to supply you with a

64

roadmap that has all of the shortcuts marked off and pitfalls cautioned, so that your road is easier than theirs.

So far, I'm going on five years on my journey. It took me five years of dedicated work, daily, to finally truly believe that I'm worth more than what I was doing and who I was pretending to be. Wow! It's been a five-year life-affirming marathon for me to really become who I am and to keep fighting for more.

You now know a bit of my story, and I shared it with you to illustrate that everyone walks in with different challenges. You know, someone might walk in with having served a prison sentence; someone might walk in that having been street homeless and a complete financial failure; some might have battled addictions and abandoned their kids, and they feel like crap about that; or maybe someone has spent their whole life thinking that they were never good enough or smart enough to achieve anything worthwhile. The majority of us are walking around deeply wounded in some way, and we carry burdens around in our own minds that don't serve us at all.

What can people change no matter what their past is or what their circumstances are? Their mindset. The words they choose to feed themselves with that allows them to see challenges themselves, their relationships and all of the world in a certain way.

When you change your words, you shift your mindset, and that empowers you to put your past in the past and move forward. What's stopping you from making that shift right now?

Choosing Better Words

Here is one gift I'd like to pass on to you, and I hope you accept it and take action on it. Tomorrow morning: The first thing in the morning, as soon as you wake up, within the first fifteen minutes—praise yourself. Acknowledge the things that are good about you, and really take it all in. Be a little selfish, a little boastful, a little self-absorbed. Then, give yourself grace—for your mistakes, for what you've messed up and forgive yourself. Believe you deserve forgiveness from yourself.

Next, choose three or four incredibly motivating, powerful words that you will say to yourself, know that you're worth it, that you deserve it and that you will put more in, and you're ready to do the work to shift your mindset throughout your day.

Be mindful in your day and be aware when your mindset shifts to old habits of self-defeat, self-criticism, self-doubt, underestimation, and be prepared to take a deliberate moment to re-frame your words and mindset into one that's more empowered, positive and compassionate.

Challenge yourself when you wake up in the morning to set yourself up for success for the rest of the day because the road ahead will beat you up if you're not ready for it.

TAKE ACTION: The Power of Words

Journal: Set a time during the day for quiet reflection. This might be a mid-day break or just before bed—some time that will allow you to think, feel and journal with some degree of peacefulness. The only time this doesn't work so well is in the

66

morning because you'll want to be able to recall the words you used throughout the day and the energy that came with them.

Reflect on any times when you might have been upset during the day: traffic, an email or other communication that annoyed you, some sad or scary news you received or just a conflict or problem that's weighing on you. List some of these issues, then next to them, list words you've used while dealing with them—these might be words you've said to other people, words you've written or just words that you've expressed in your head that never escaped your lips, but you thought them.

Write those down, then read them over. Next, think about how those words made you feel. Were they the best words to use at that moment? What energy did you give them? How have they impacted your mindset? How have they impacted your relationships? And, frankly, do you owe anyone apologies for the words you used?

Now, think about better word choices. If you could replace certain words and phrases, what words would you use instead: empowering, compassionate, kind, helpful, direct words. List those and feel how using these new words reshape your mindset.

It might seem tedious, but if you listen closely, many highly successful people use a different vocabulary than everyone else. It's a vocabulary of possibility, grace, kindness and abundance. Without taking action to consciously change the words you use throughout your day, your mindset will remain stuck and resistant to change.

CHAPTER 5: Believe in Yourself

When a person begins to believe in themselves, many parts of their life become aligned. For some people, these parts of their lives align because they began to believe in themselves, and for others, because they started aligning these things in their lives, they began believing in themselves. And, just to clarify, when we're talking about someone believing in themselves—we're not talking about some imaginary things becoming real like the tooth fairy, right? What we are talking about is a cluster of psychological strengths building up and coming together such as self-worth, self-confidence, self-esteem and self-love. With this psychological healing, awakening and strength-building are these specific life areas that are intricately connected, and they are: health, relationships, finances, career and spirituality. As the psychological end strengthens, so do these life areas, and as the life areas strengthen, so do the psychological areas.

As obvious as this might seem to many, the complexity is in taking purposeful, impactful and consistent action to strengthen these areas. Nearly everyone is struggling with one or more of these issues, and likely there are even some challenging habits and repeating toxic thought processes that need to be broken and re-framed to overcome barriers for success.

At the core of this is that you must believe in yourself—you must believe that you are worthy of experiencing the changes in your life that you seek. You must believe that you have the strength and ability to make these changes to experience a more fulfilled and purposeful life. You must believe in yourself to know that while making these changes in your life might get hard at times, you have the confidence and power to make the changes stick, that your hard work will pay off and you can experience profound, sustained change.

For me, I was empowered by my faith in God, and that gave me the strength I needed to begin believing in myself which was especially critical in a time of my life where I felt the lowest, the most worthless, the most unworthy. It was believing that I'm worth something to God that allowed me to have the strength in the first place to step up and begin believing in myself. My first steps towards self-worth at that period of my life stemmed from a belief that I was meant to do more than what I'm doing with my life. That was huge for me.

Believing that I was meant for more, and that I have—that we all have—all of these gifts that we have to use is a powerful driving force. I felt to my core like I wasn't doing what I was called to do, but the feeling that *I was called to do something* allowed me to take my first steps towards believing in myself.

What Is Good About You?

The very next step in believing in yourself is to decide what is good about you. Again, in theory, this likely seems very simple, but it can get a little more complex when you have to actually do it sometimes. Let me just simply ask you, "What is good about you?"

If you can sit down right now and easily and comfortably rattle off about 20 or more things that you know to be good about you, then you're in pretty good shape. But I'll be honest with you, if you had asked me this question about five years ago, I would have paused for a long time before responding at all. Then I would have finally, responded: "I think I'm a good person," without any degree of confidence in my answer.

71

Here's a little insight, too—if you are having a difficult time with listing the things that are good about you, it is because your limiting beliefs are beating you up right now in your head. You've handed them the wheel, and these limiting beliefs are now driving your self-worth, self-confidence, and self-esteem. I'll invite you right now to take back control of that wheel and start driving your own race car.

It's important not to discount the power those limiting beliefs hold over you. For me those feelings of self-doubt and unworthiness reach up at most unexpected times and toss me around. They can cause you to regress on all the progress you've made with your personal development, and they can make you become someone that you're not.

Your limiting beliefs take over, and they try to tell you that's who you are, and that's all you're meant to be until you start to change your words and change your mindset and surround yourself with people who are motivating, holding you accountable and coaching you. So if you ask me now what's good about me? I'm the person who wants to better myself every single day, and I focus on every area of my life every single day to become a better version of me so I can be a better version for everybody that comes into contact with me—so that I can make an impact on others and be of service.

This is a good time to activate your journal. I encourage you to actually create a list answering the question, "What is good about me?"

In the beginning, this list is going to look very different than when you've gone through extensive personal development lessons like the ones presented in this book, but that's the

72

point—to assess where you are right now and capture a clear picture of your current state of mind and self-worth.

It's okay if you only have two or three or a couple of dozen. If you find this task challenging, please know that it's truly understandable, and you're not alone. When you're not feeling so great about yourself, and you've heard messages throughout your life that you're not good enough, and you've been let down and you feel like you're always letting others down, this task is difficult, and that makes it oh so much more important.

The best gift you could give yourself if you're struggling right now is to engage the services of a life or business coach or a mentor to guide you through exploring everything that's good about you, and I already know that there is so much good about you. Seriously, here are a few things I can tell you that are good about you right now: you invest in personal development; you're hopeful; you believe in the power of change; and you strive to better yourself. I know these things about you for a fact just because you've invested your time into reading this book!

Engaging a coach will help you identify 15 more qualities that are good about you, and there's a reason this is important work, and why it's important to complete it even if it seems a bit challenging—or especially if it seems a bit challenging. Once you allow yourself to not only see the good in yourself, but to identify specific qualities about you that are good and abundant, it gets really hard for those limiting beliefs to take over and lie to you, telling you you're someone you're not. Building this ammunition is critical to fighting those battles when they arise, and you will be the victor every time!

As a coach, when I do this exercise with my clients, it's really astounding for them if all they could come up with on their own were a couple things on their list. I already know a little about them, so I start by asking them questions I already know a little about to get them to list things that are good about them: maybe it's their career and income, maybe it's their loving family, maybe it's the beautiful way they treat others, their volunteer work, the way they care for their health, maybe it's their home or nice car, etc.

Then I have them look over their new list and have them think about this incredible person who has all of these good qualities about them. Then I ask them, would you want to be in a relationship with that person? And they say, "Oh, yeah." Would you like to do business with that person, "Sure— absolutely," they reply.

Then I say, "Well, that's you!" Their initial list started with two to four things, and in working with them, we now have a list of 15 – 20, a list of true and actual things about them that makes them "good"—character traits, achievements, material things, successes, all they've been through, and their gifts.... Then I say, "I want to describe a person to you, and you tell me what you think about this person." Tell me if you'd like to have a relationship with this person. Then, I tell them a story about a person—their story about themselves being a bright, accomplished, loving, worthy, successful person. Facts.

Beyond Your Limiting Beliefs: Self-love

Beyond the land of believing in yourself is a destination of even greater beauty and strength, and this is the place of self-love. I will tell you that it's impossible to reach this place until you've first purchased some real estate in the land of believing in yourself, but self-love is the next stop on the evolution of the journey, and it's nothing short of magical.

Self-love is all about relationships, but what you realize quickly is that the most important relationship that you will ever have in your life is with yourself. If you don't nurture that relationship properly, all other relationships in your life don't have a proper foundation to keep everything grounded and steady. It's the difference between building a house on a slab of poured concrete or soft sand. That sand is not stable—it's going to shift and slide causing the house to crack and crumble with the slightest kind of disruption. The house that was built on a concrete foundation, however, is sturdy, and it will serve as a solid, protective sanctuary for all when even heavy storms rage.

When you love yourself, you're emotionally healthy. When you're emotionally healthy, you are able to be a support to others when they need you while not having to get sucked into the turmoil yourself. You can stand strong when challenges arise in life that strain communication, tempers run hot and feelings are fragile. When you love yourself, your foundation keeps you grounded in hope, problem-solving, and pouring light into darkness. You lead with grace and compassion versus fear and insecurity, and that allows everyone around you to have a safe place with you to heal, grow and flourish.

Self-love is so very important, and like most things in life that are important, it doesn't come easily. There's some work involved because in this area of personal development, we are constantly evolving. When you've reached one level, there's even more brilliance of it to experience up ahead, and that's the bliss of evolving in self-love. Even if we have been blessed with a beautiful amount of self-love, there's always

75

more to explore and develop. I, however, was not so lucky. Self-love was as foreign to me as a distant planet in another solar system. Of course, I didn't realize that at first. Relationships kept failing, and I couldn't understand why all the love I poured into the other person just wasn't enough. Well, there is some truth to the saying, "You can't love anyone else until you love yourself first." Don't get caught up on that and take it too literally—it's not entirely true—but in this context, it has merit. Let me explain…

I was raised to put the other person first in relationships. My needs, wants and values weren't as much of a priority as theirs, so at every turn, my focus was on caring for them. While that might sound nice to hear, it's a disaster in practice. First of all, you can't respect a person who doesn't respect themselves, and you can't respect yourself when you're putting everyone else ahead of you. And as many of us have experienced, relationships devoid of respect are doomed. I was the poster child for this scenario spanning many girlfriends and five failed marriages.

My general scenario went like this: I would love on that person like crazy. I would love them so hard, but if I didn't feel like I received love back the way that I expected it, I would feel beat down, unloved and really unlovable. I would try so hard to make the other person happy so that they would love me, and when it turns out that they weren't happy or they didn't love me the way I expected it or they'd take their frustrations out on me, it would eat me up. I'd spiral into thinking what's wrong with me, why don't they love me, why are they always so angry and unhappy with me, and I'd just feel like I wasn't worth it, and I'd give up eventually.

If I had any degree of self-love at the time, things wouldn't have played out that way. I'd make sure I was fulfilled first,

76

not relying on the approval, love and happiness from my partner to make me feel loved and worthy of love. Their unhappiness and anger wouldn't have had such a deep impact on my self-worth because through self-love, I'd already know that I'm more than worthy of love, and I'd be able to accept love more freely, too, without being so suspicious of it because I know I'm deserving of it. Today I know that it's okay to love someone without staking all of my self-worth on them loving me back. I can love people because that's who I am, not because I want or expect or need something back in return.

Thinking You Can / Deciding You Must

Michael Jordan, yes, the NBA star Jordan, has famously said, "I've missed more than 9,000 shots in my career. I've lost almost 300 games. Twenty-six times, I've been trusted to take the game winning shot and missed. I've failed over and over and over again in my life, and that is why I succeed."

Jordan's commitment to the game of basketball is second to none, as reported by literally everyone who has ever seen him in action from his high school coach through college and onto the professional court, Jordan was the best because he literally worked harder, longer and was more committed than any other player. Failures didn't stop him—they propelled him. What would happen if we applied even a fraction of that level of commitment to any area of our lives? I'll give you the answer: success.

When we start anything new and expect to be successful at it, there's usually a process to it. First, we'll be excited by it, because it's something we really want to do. Then we try it, and since we're new to it, we're probably not very good at it.

77

Right here is the moment of truth. Do we keep going and push through the hard work it's going to take to get good at it, or are we going to stop, decide we're not very good at it and give up? This is actually a thought pattern that most of us form when we're very young, and we start making decisions about life. Do we just try something, see if we're good at it and if not, give up? Or, do we commit to doing something and learning it, practicing hard until we get good at it and allow our failures to propel us to work harder and get even better?

Do you think you can, know that you will or decide that you must? Each of these are actually about determining your level of commitment. How much do you want change and results in your life? What decisions and levels of commitment are you willing to make to achieve that change and those results?

Often, we may start with thinking, okay, I think I can make this leap. I think change is possible. But just by using that vocabulary, you're telling your brain you're not committed to anything. If it gets hard, or you're too busy, or something distracts you or you lose interest, you don't really need to follow-through. After all, you were just "trying" it. Making a decision to actually commit to a powerful change in our lives, shifts our language to "I will". Now, decision aligns with action and commitment, and change begins to take place— you're committed to push through the challenges, to refocus when you get distracted, and to get back up when you fail and keep going. The next level in commitment is deciding that "you must". Now, your decision has an implied consequence—you must put in the extra hard work, stay focused, propel through failure because not doing so is not an option.

The power of our word choices can't be overlooked. Our words are hard-wired to our brains—when we think them, say them, write them—they create energy and patterns that transform mindset and trigger actions. Your commitment to change is directly related to your mindset and therefore your word choices.

I've said to so many people, from girlfriends to parents to people at my job, if I ever say, "I can't" or "I'll try" or "I might", if I were to ever, ever say something like that, they have been asked to look me right in the eye and tell me to change my words. As I was getting into the coaching industry, I became a free coach to all my employees and my son and everybody in my life who was interested, so they are each very aware of their words, and you will hardly ever hear one of them slip up and say the words, "I can't." Eradicating those limiting beliefs is tied to your words, and your decisions and commitment are charged by your words. Be mindful about what you're saying, how you're saying it and your level of commitment towards the things that matter in your life.

Do you want to achieve profound and lasting change, high performance and ultimate success? Then you must commit to it. You have no other choice if you're going to get what you want.

TAKE ACTION: Believe in Yourself

Visualization: Set just one goal right now—something that is achievable, and you can see progress as you improve. Make sure that it is something that will benefit from practice, routine and commitment at getting better. This could be weight loss, an improved time running 3 miles, improving time management at work to boost performance, improving

79

your relationship with your spouse or kids by spending more time with them, having fun, and making them feel special to you, etc.

Now, visualize the work that you put in leading to the improved outcome, and experience, in your mind, what ultimate success in that area would feel like. Hold that in your head for a few minutes to truly let it seep into your consciousness.

Remember, when you start this change, it might not go perfectly, and that is specifically why you're making a commitment to it so that gradually it will improve with consistency and practice. You are visualizing so that you can attach the energy of success to the routine you're building. Habits form only when there is momentum, and the quickest way to build that momentum is by attaching positive emotions to the routine you're building from the start before you actually experience change in that area.

Take Action: Begin the new habits that will lead to you achieving your identified goal. You might want to consider letting the people around you know what you're up to if it might involve them or if they'll see you implementing this new change. Ask them for their support, and you may even ask them to help hold you accountable while reminding them that it's new to you, so you won't be perfect at it right away.

CHAPTER 6: Gratitude the Lifestyle

Leading Your Thought Processes

Before I could really appreciate who I was becoming or the people around me, I really struggled with my self-esteem. Believing in yourself is so often overlooked as the greatest barrier to any form of self-improvement. Do you even deserve to change? Are you a good enough person, smart enough, talented enough, valued enough to really be valuable in the world? Do you even have what it takes within you to achieve lasting, powerful change? Or, are you just going to fail and fold on this like you have most everything that's been challenging in your life? Will you just be ridiculed and humiliated if you start to make positive changes in your life, and you don't succeed right away?

I learned that the most powerful place to start, as a person who struggled with massively low self-esteem, is in a space of gratitude. I began by finding immense gratitude for everything I had within me at any given moment—my breath, my heart, my faith, my goodness, my commitment to be better for others, the love and many gifts that have been placed in my life…

That's where I came up with the first part of my personal mantra of "*Blessed and Unstoppable*". I'm truly blessed, and my sense of self-esteem bloomed from that feeling of being immensely blessed. I want to honor and be grateful for where I am in my life no matter where that might be. That might sound weird when you consider that at some point I was living out of my car. At another part I was driving over a bridge, and it crossed my mind to maybe drive over the edge because everything felt so bleak and hopeless. How can you feel grateful and blessed in moments like that, and I'll tell you that these moments are exactly when you need to reach in and find your blessings and gratitude more than at any other time in your life. Finding gratitude in your darkest days gives you the opportunity to wake up in the morning and feel blessed no matter what.

Your dark moment in life is the moment when you are finally open to profound change. People don't dig deep within themselves and go through the agony of soul-level transformation when things are going great. They do this work when they know that a full transformation is their only lifeline back to sanity and success (however one defines their personal success). It really comes down to a level of brokenness—to be readied for a state of profound change, you have to be broken.

We need to be broken to the point where we feel we have no other choice but to change—to go through the process: pain, failure, hard work and commitment, realizing incremental improvement and then ultimately success. That state of brokenness is unique to each individual to define by their own measure, too. It could be a void in their relationships, a loss of loved ones and support, prison or homelessness, losing fortunes or just feeling suffocated in the everydayness of an uninspired and unintentional life.

For me, I had to get to the point where I was like, man, I had nothing that made me feel okay; I seemed to fail at everything that mattered to me; I was a walking disappointment to myself and everyone around me. Still, I had and still have my faith. I'm grateful for that. I mean, I'm truly grateful! I was raised in a family that told me to put God first. Even if I didn't believe at the time when I was younger, I always carried my faith with me, and it just got stronger as I've needed something bigger than myself to turn to and believe in, especially when I found it impossible to believe in myself.

Defining Success

I was just talking to a client who's a multi-millionaire, and by most people's standards, he's wildly successful. However, he's totally miserable. He has no support system and no one in his fife that he trusts. Everyone that he's ever trusted has turned on him and stabbed him in the back. He feels like he's an inch tall. Of course, to most people looking in, they think this guy is amazing and has it all together, and yet, he's just a heartbeat away from crying all the time because he feels like everything has fallen out from under him.

If all you cared about to define success for yourself was the big mansion and the car—great, he's all set. But when the people you loved and trusted and you tried to protect and provide for betray you, that's not a good feeling. Your bottom falls out, and you're heartbroken, fearing to trust anyone again. When you're in crisis, that sense of gratitude is really hard to find when you feel so small and unlovable, regardless of how you might be perceived outwardly.

The question to think about is this: where does 90 percent of the world turn to when they reach a point of despair—void of any success or hope? Usually, the answer is either drugs or God.

There's a well-known story from the famous motivational speaker, Les Brown, where he talks about the best and worst day of his life. He was so excited to deliver the biggest speech of his life, at that point, to a huge audience. The audience is hyped up—they are even chanting for him. The energy is electric, and Les calls his wife when he's backstage during a break. He's found the most supportive woman of his dreams who would tell him thinks like: You're going to be the best motivational speaker in the world; I believe in you, etc.

84

Reportedly, Les said something to his wife like: "Hey, here's what they're yelling for me, 'We want the motivator. We want the motivator...' They're yelling at me, screaming."

She tells him that she hears it. Then, Les says he heard someone in the background saying something like: "Get off the phone. Get back here."

Long story short, this is the moment when Les's wife informs him that she wants a divorce. He then has to go back on stage and complete the most important day of his career.

He was telling his wife about the most exciting part of his life, and a moment later, he finds himself simultaneously in the most broken part of his life. He still has to go out and give one of the best speeches of his life, no matter what else he's feeling. In our broken times, we still have to do what we have to do.

Success is a hard thing to deliver consistently if we make it about us because we're easily swayed by our moods and external circumstances. When success becomes about us, and we become broken, we can't go out there. But it's not about us, we are driven by a greater purpose, our "Why", that keeps us on course. For Les, in that moment, it was probably about his commitment to the people in that audience and even the commitment he made to himself as a professional, and that's what drove him to go back out when he felt like crumbling.

If you think about that story of Les Brown's, you can probably feel the pain he was in, as most of us have been in a similar circumstance at some point in our lives. We know what it feels like to have our stomach jump up to our throat. Emotional pain and anxiety grip you. You can't breathe. And

85

now you must get it together to go perform and pretend that emotional upset didn't even happen. You must put that away and go do your job.

Not everyone knows how to compartmentalize and set their feelings aside to go do something. Plus, the skill of compartmentalization doesn't always work in our favor either. It can make us appear cold-hearted and it forces us to delay dealing with emotional pain—sometimes indefinitely which causes deep problems with unresolved grief, pain or trauma.

So God bless Les for having the gift to experience great heartbreak and to be able to say, "Not now; I'll deal with that later."

Knowing Your "Why"

Knowing that your "Why"—why you are driven to do what you do—it is so much bigger than you. It drives you to push through the hardest challenges and barriers. When I discovered my "Why"—my purpose—I realized that all of the things that used to propel me fell flat because it wasn't about me anymore. Instead, it was about me becoming the best version of me that I can be for "YOU". It was about fulfilling God's purpose for me, and I quickly realize that if I don't go back out there onto that stage like Les Brown did, I'm not letting me down, I'm letting down all of the people that came here to see me and I'm letting down my greater purpose.

This then comes full circle back to gratitude, realizing that you are there to serve the people who are depending on you to step out on that stage even when you don't want to. So, it's not only your clients who you might have a certain rapport with, and they might forgive your need to reschedule for personal reasons, but in Les's case, people paid him to be on that stage, and others paid to see you on that stage. Certain words you speak on that stage can reach out and touch and even change lives. That's powerful, and it's not about you. You're just a vessel! Your purpose is much greater than your current feelings.

Putting your feelings aside to deliver your purpose-driven work is an act of gratitude and humbleness on a high level. It's about learning that your ego is not part of this scenario so you can box up your problems for now because there's something bigger here.

The Journey of Gratitude

To begin finding that place of pure gratitude within you, it's best to start by planting a seed. Pick out one area in your life and write five things that are good about you. It's funny that the first time I ask someone to write down something positive about themselves, something good about themselves, they usually write down one or two things and struggle with the third one and so on. Then they often get emotional and start crying. I support them through the process, then after four or five sessions, they can finally start listing ten to fifteen good things about themselves.

The journey isn't so much painful as it is frustrating when you begin. Most of us are taught not to brag about ourselves, not to boast or speak too highly of ourselves, and all of that is good advice, of course. It's insufferable to listen to someone go on and on about how amazing they are all of the time— they sound self-absorbed and like an ego maniac. However,

87

over-application of not being boastful seems to be as detrimental to our personal development. This is when we downgrade our positive traits so much so that we have difficulty identifying them in our own lives. It buries our self-esteem and self-awareness so that we find it hard to draw from our strengths because we're not even fully aware of what they are. That's why this process is so important and a beginning step to becoming the best version of you.

Gratitude begins as an internal journey, so start by just finding two or three things to be grateful for about yourself in your life. Then really focus in on those, lifting those up in your view of yourself. Next, begin being grateful for others in your life, lifting people up around you. Being grateful for the people in your life that you know helps them become a better version of themselves even while you're in your broken state.

We normally don't think to help others when we feel ourselves broken because when you're in a broken state you think you can't help anybody else. However, in doing so, that's when gratitude and purpose enter your heart. You might feel worthless, but when you find out that you are worth something by helping someone else become better through whatever you're doing, your self-esteem jolts up. You find that suddenly you have some value, and gratitude shows up for you.

It's not unusual for therapists to recommend that their clients who are dealing with depression volunteer somewhere. Of course, this is not in place of medication or other therapies, but in addition to those, some patients find that actively volunteering where they can give of themselves to help others and see the impact they have made is powerfully therapeutic. They can feel a sense of their own gratitude bubble up just through the act of doing something for someone else. It

88

doesn't need to be big: mowing a neighbor's lawn, helping a senior with chores, etc. It might seem small and insignificant to you, but it might mean the world to someone else.

Volunteer to help someone else, and watch what that does for you and your sense of gratitude. The impact can spread, passing along feelings of gratitude to others and even for yourself. So, going through the thought process of gratitude, volunteering to help people, giving of yourself and your gifts or even just time, compassion and helpfulness is an important way to live in a state of gratitude. Also, the activity of listing qualities that are good about yourself puts you into a state of gratitude. Then just journaling on things that in general you're grateful for in your life. These are all things that any person can do to really embark on a lifestyle of gratitude.

I reached a point in my life where I was so broken that I had to do everything in my power to start believing in myself. As we discussed, it's nearly impossible to have any kind of gratitude when you just have no self-esteem. It all starts with you, in your head, in your thoughts and beliefs. It begins by being grateful for who you are, that you are alive with whatever gifts and positive qualities you possess in your heart. Then you find gratitude in what blessings you have—maybe it's the people around you or even some of your possessions, or a job, a church family or any number of things. Eventually, you find your way to being grateful for your experiences because whatever they are, they've molded you to be the person you are. No matter how broken you feel, you've been resilient enough to get through it—you're still here. Plus, you learned some things that you can now use to help propel you to transform and become your best version of you.

This isn't easy. Being grateful for what's gone on in your life when you don't really feel so grateful about your life is hard.

89

However, going through this process leads you to knowing what you're meant for, knowing that you're meant for more than what you're doing and your current state of being. You delve into deep feelings through this process, and often you need to get out of your feelings—negative feelings—to begin healing and moving forward in gratitude. Feelings of shame, worthlessness, anger, hurt, fear, resentment, bitterness, vindictiveness, guilt, sadness, contempt—all of these feelings will keep you stuck in brokenness, and you owe it to yourself and to the world around you that needs your gifts, to release yourself from the grip of these feelings. They don't serve you in any positive way, and they do no harm nor hold any power over anyone but you. You deserve the gift of freeing yourself from the burden of your own pain.

As a coach, when I work with my clients through this process, the goal truly is about living in gratitude. That's where all of the big healing happens. You can't hold anger, shame and resentment in the same space with gratitude. Gratitude won't let you do that; she's a very possessive spirit, and she won't share with any negativity. However, she'll happily share space with love, grace, compassion, joy, peace, kindness, etc.

Also, when we dig in so deep into our negative feelings, that's where we forget about all of our own positive traits, all of the things we do well and all of the good things about ourselves. Our self-esteem tanks, and we literally lose who we are, what our purpose in life is meant to be, what we value most and the good things that drive us to succeed, overcome and transform.

As a coach, it's up to me to replenish your sense of self-worth and gratitude, to help you realize that you have done some great things in your life and have amazing qualities that are so

90

valuable and needed. The pain you've lived through was just a chapter in your life that you now get to use to propel you forward, but you also get to pass through it and write a new chapter. As we process through this, as a coach, I help you to recall the other chapters in your life where you proved to yourself that you were incredible, where you saved yourself, where you helped others, even changed lives. When we pull these memories out, gratitude enters in.

It's always a great idea to get a mentor or a coach to help guide you through this. If you're "white knuckling" it for some reason on your own, I hope that you are at least using a book like this or some other book or program to use as a guide. Not because this is terribly complex, but because following a structured and guided approach to this work will make the journey shorter and less painful, but more importantly because it will be more impactful and lasting. You can clearly see the chain reaction from gratitude to mindset to personal development to success. You'll also see the intense barriers created by negative thought processes and how to identify each rapidly throughout your day, avoiding setbacks and staying focused on growth.

Nothing about this process is passive. You can't set an autopilot or cruise control and just sit and observe. It's a treacherous terrain that requires your full concentration, quick thinking and hard work. If it was easy, everyone would be doing it, and we'd have a planet full of happy, peaceful, compassionate, successful people filled with gratitude. Most people live in a mindset far off course from that description, so if you want to be different, there are no shortcuts. You must put in the dedication and work.

Picking Up the Pieces

Life will always serve up some massively hard times. There is no escaping it—from abuses, heartbreak and extreme loss of loved ones to disasters, loss of security and even complete ruin--life can beat us up so badly that we're not sure we'll ever survive it. Yet if we're still here, we did indeed survive it. Then what? The next step is to pick up the pieces and decide which ones to discard, which ones to use and how exactly to use them.

When we discover which pieces to keep and take with us, those are the bits that we took something out of to better ourselves and to grow from. Truly we grow far more from pain and failure than we ever will from success. Our most teachable moments are when we are sitting in the messiness of life, and we take the time to examine what went wrong. We must take responsibility for our mistakes and failures; we accept the grief and catastrophe handed to us; we move past betrayals, abuse and injustice, and we decide that after taking some time to heal, we must find a way to move on. We do this through gratitude.

No, no one is asking you to be grateful for what happened. It would be monstrous to ask you to be grateful for the death of a loved one, for financial ruin, for the collapse of your business, or for your heartbreak. Gratitude enters in when you take inventory of all that is good, loving, helpful, supportive and strong during and/or after the breaking point. When you shift your focus out of the gripping agony that left you broken and onto the life that is still left in front of you to live, gratitude is there. In this way, gratitude is your ultimate healer.

Let's focus on the concept of failure for a moment. When we take responsibility for our part in something that went wrong, we often classify that as failure. We failed—we did something or didn't do something that directly impacted something to go very wrong. One question—after you accepted responsibility for your part in something that went wrong, what did you learn from it?

Did it ever happen again? Could it happen again? How did you change or what did you do to prevent the problem from recurring?

Whatever your answers to those questions are, chances are that you learned a lot from it. In some cases, you might have learned never to do that thing again. If it was a bad habit or a toxic mindset that led to the problem, you might not have been able to correct it immediately, but still you learned from it. You recognized the problem you created, so now you can identify it more easily and work to avoid causing similar harm in most cases even if you haven't irradicated the problem in yourself all together.

If the problem existed because of someone else or circumstances beyond your control, how better can you protect yourself and the problem from recurring? How can you mitigate the risk of future similar problems?

When you fully understand what you overcame and how, the introspection of it and the changes you made to overcome your obstacle, you find yourself in that space of gratitude.

When I work with clients as their coach, I can guarantee that we can list at least 15 things that are good about them. We often begin the process by focusing on the one thing that they know happened maybe 10, 15 years ago, five years ago that they did or experienced that just tore them up. The thing that they said they would never do or go through again. Always, something from that experience helped change their life, profoundly. Whatever that was, there was something there that they remember was a critical change for them.

For instance, a client might say to me "And my ex-boyfriend cheated on me" or "He could never hold down a job; I was always supporting us." They just start talking and telling their story.

I listen, then I repeat back to them what they said to me, paraphrased, "So what you just said to me is that what you went through with that boyfriend, you promised yourself you would never let that happen again. And ever since then, you went for a different kind of guy. So, it's pretty incredible now that you know you're worth more than what you had in him, and you'll never settle for that again."

They find a place of gratitude that they first went through the pain, learned from it, accepted their responsibility for the part they played, and then they changed something about themselves to prevent the problem from recurring. A part of that included self-love.

Too often, we think that these things that are good about us and all that we've overcome aren't significant because while painful or difficult, they just seemed like ordinary things that people just go through. That's exactly the point! The changes might seem small, but they are far from insignificant. They aren't meant to be glanced over but to be acknowledged and celebrated—that's gratitude.

If we coast through life stuck on autopilot, relying on our cruise control, and we don't pay attention to the little things,

94

that is how we get stuck. That is the formula for ensuring a slow and arduous path towards personal development if any personal development will occur at all. Yet when we shift our focus onto the little things, the small wins, the positive adjustments and solutions—our new focus will set us on a path towards achieving more of those wins, adjustments and solutions. We'll begin to see opportunities for these to happen everywhere, in all areas of our life, with gratitude. That is the real formula for success.

Gratitude and Being Humble

Another path towards gratitude has to do with staying humble. Humbleness is so important because when you can humble yourself in front of someone, you guys can both humble yourselves. It's not about who wins anymore, who's right or wrong. If you stay humble, you can communicate better. Without that, your communication style can get all jacked up because you're both trying to win or to prove that one is right and the other is wrong. However, when you learn to humble yourself, everything starts to change because the goal is not to be right or prove the other person wrong— the goal is to better understand where the other person is coming from, how they feel, what they are afraid of and how to come to a solution.

At its core, the whole point of it is that I just want to love you. However, when we're angry about something, and those emotions are getting the better of us, we're not able to communicate effectively. If we both learn to humble ourselves and we both hold gratitude for each other, we can overcome the temporary flare up of anger. We can remember that you value this person and your relationship with them. Then, you can engage in a conversation about a heated issue.

95

CHAPTER 7: Compassionate Leadership

What Top Companies Are Seeking

In business, and this applies to all areas of our life as well, we have classifications of hard skills and soft skills. Hard skills are the things that you were taught and you know how to do like how to be an engineer, how to be a doctor, how to balance your books, how to market and advertise, etc. In life, they would be things like how to cook, clean and pay your bills on time, how to maintain a car or a house, how to host a holiday dinner and all of those skills. On the other hand, there are soft skills. These are "people skills" and things that you bring to the table that you really can't teach someone. In work, those would be how to coach an employee to better engage with them at work, how to listen to a frustrated team member or customer to put them at ease, how to be proactive in your communication so that your team can best support you and the goals of your project, etc. In life, those soft skills would include how to listen with compassion, how to manage conflict, how to show love and support to others and so forth.

In this book, we talk a lot about the soft skills of gratitude, about being blessed and unstoppable and about being humble. Compassion is another top skill that is far too often overlooked, especially in the workplace, and that's a huge misstep. Because when you lead with compassion it rewards everybody, and it sets the stage for a culture of gratitude.

Compassionate leadership isn't just a nice thing to do, or some term I just made up to fit an agenda—leaders of major corporations have published articles and emphasized in interviews that this is the top soft skill that they value.

These companies are looking for job candidates who demonstrate compassion. They want to hire leaders that have this sense and compassion so that they know they're going to treat the people that work for them well. Companies have learned that when employees are treated with a little bit of heart and not just as a function for input and output, productivity levels grow and so does morale and loyalty.

Employees are an investment to a company—it costs money to recruit, hire and train an employee. Plus, once they have been there a while, their experience in the company culture, the synergy they have developed with a team and many other benefits that are difficult to quantify are a huge asset to a company. Good employees are not easily replaceable, but far too many companies steeped in an outdated and toxic corporate culture of "no one is special and you're only as good as your last performance" make people feel undervalued and demoralized.

However, when a leader leads with compassion, it is an understanding that life happens, and that sometimes we have to work through things. People are not always on top of their game or performing their best for a variety of reasons, and a compassionate leader will open a dialogue and make some accommodations to allow a valuable employee to work through their issue for a time. Everything from serious illnesses in the family to divorce and childcare problems and many more issues can have a negative impact on work performance, but most often these issues are short lived. If a compassionate leader can make temporary accommodations such as flexible work schedules, work from home options, even temporary reassignment of some responsibilities, it will go a long way to relieve stress for the employee along with building trust, morale and loyalty.

When we think about the concepts of gratitude and what it takes for a person to believe in themselves, we need to remember that as leaders, we have some influence over this.

If we have the authority to build people up, then we also have the power to tear them down, and that is a potentially dangerous power to have over another person. It's a responsibility in leadership that we must take very seriously, because how we treat others determines not only the culture that we create for them, but it also defines who we are and what we value.

What Does Compassion Look Like?

When we think about other people and how we approach them, how we treat them, compassion requires us to present ourselves with a degree of empathy. That is, we must take a moment to understand what another person is feeling and going through before we respond to a situation with them. This is in alignment with gratitude—when we lead with gratitude, we'll see this other person as valuable, and it will be natural for us to care about what they might be going through that led them to be in a bad mood or to perform poorly at work. When you choose to approach this person with compassion, when you choose to care about them versus judging them or wanting to punish them, that is the spark that can change the trajectory of everything in the moment.

This is what major corporations are seeking in their leaders above all other qualities. They know that they can teach just about anyone policies and procedures. They can read your resume, ask you some questions and check your references to see that you're qualified to do the job. What sets leaders apart is if they know how to treat other people compassionately.

The one thing that I disagree with in this whole push towards hiring and promoting compassionate leaders is this idea that a skill like this cannot be taught. Granted, some people might

100

be resistant to the idea of becoming a compassionate leader, and in that case, it probably can't be taught. The old mindset of "it's my way or the highway" leadership isn't going to easily transition into compassionate leadership, but that's not the average leader. The average leader is generally open to self-improvement, to learning new skills and effective leadership techniques. I believe the average leader can absolutely be taught to become a compassionate leader, but it's not a passive process.

What if every leader had to take part in personal development coaching to become a better leader, to be hired as a leader and to be promoted as a leader? I'd completely advocate for this. I took coaching lessons to become a better coach because my investment equals my success. It only makes sense that leaders would take part in coaching to perform as better leaders or that companies would invest in such training. If you can learn the skill of leading compassionately, to elevate the self-esteem and empowerment of your workforce, if they see that you care beyond their productivity, you foster a healthier, more committed and loyal workforce.

Through compassionate leadership, you also acknowledge that different people respond better to different communication styles. Right? Everybody has issues that they carry with them. I don't care how many people you're dealing with or how old they are. People are all carrying baggage with them that will cause them to respond differently to different styles of communication. Even the phrasing that is used matters. Expert copywriters will tell you that there are key phrases that will automatically turn off a number of readers, so don't use those phrases or you'll lose readers before you even tell them what problems you're solving. Some of these phrases are: 1) let me break this down; 2) let me explain; 3) you see; 4) let's face it; 5) chances are; 6) listen, and so on.

101

Why are these key phrases problematic? Because they give an air of being condescending. The same is true in conversation—focus on how the message will be received. Speak to the people you're communicating with as your team, as valuable, intelligent partners who want to succeed along with you.

Compassionate leaders actually do think about the feelings of the people they're leading because being a great leader is about lifting people up around you. The old view of leadership is that "I'm up here and you're down there, so you will do as I say." They believe that since they are in charge, they can leave early and have everyone else do the hard work without you pitching in because you're the leader.

But we've learned through time that this doesn't create the best workforce or team—it's demoralizing, and people would rather put their energy somewhere else where they feel valued than to put up with that nonsense. There are other jobs, other teams and other leaders. Valuable team members can find an environment that is committed to lifting up their teams, and it's far more rewarding to be a part of that culture than one that treats everyone as though they are easily replaceable.

In one of my current jobs, I operate a gym, which includes managing about 56 employees with the youngest person being about 19 years old and the oldest is probably 60, men and women. Many have totally different jobs from a maintenance guy to team leaders to childcare workers to sales team to front desk team to personal trainers to people that teach the classes. Then, not only do they have different jobs, but they each have different personalities, sensitivities, preferences, and so to address that, I treat each one differently.

Well, someone might want to correct me and say that I need to treat everyone equally. Yes, of course, we're all equal, but we are also each very different. So it's a mindset of gratitude and compassion. You can treat everybody beautifully, but people need to hear things in a different velocity. For me, it's an exciting part of my job, to respond compassionately to my teams, but it can be an extreme learning curve for some leaders. I promise you, though, there is nothing more rewarding for you or your team.

Invest in Your Team

What makes me different than from say, who I was even five to ten years ago, is that while I was a good person and I worked with a whole lot of really good people very successfully, now I invest in their success.

I don't just work with them to be a good employee; I invest in them to be a better person, and everybody knows that. It's not about me just making them an awesome employee and making them really good at their job; I'm committed to helping them become a better person so that they reach goals in their life to achieve what it is that they want to achieve.

For example, one of my old employees who worked with me at another gym—he started working for me just before I left. I wasn't really a mentor or life coach back then, but I was a cool boss who definitely cared about my employees. He stayed in touch by following me on Facebook for about four to five years now. I saw him work at different places that I noticed. We never talked on the phone over the years, but my number never changed. So, I get a phone call at about nine o'clock at night. I'm in bed, and I hear this voice on the

103

phone say, "Hey, Hunter, what's going on? Hey, man, I just had to call you."

"Hey, what's going on?" I asked. What he said next almost made me cry.

He said to me, "Hey, brother, I had to call you. I just want to let you know that I've been following you for the last four or five years, man. And every morning when I wake up, you're the first person I go to listen to for motivational stuff. And I watch how you've changed your life over the years. And it's motivated me to change mine. And let me tell you, brother, my relationship with my wife has gotten better. I realize that life is more to than partying and having fun, and everything has changed in my life. And I want you to know that you were the one thing that started it for me."

I barely knew how to respond except with gratitude. I just wanted to be different—not just for me but for everyone around me. Now people see something different in me, and they trust me and have faith in themselves because I am dedicated every day to lift up the people around me. I take that so seriously—I work so hard at that. But my former employee and friend saw a guy that was a stripper, and now he sees me as someone drastically different. I'm still a good person, but I've truly changed the way I live my life, and I walk the walk and talk the talk. He noticed that, and it changed him.

He let me know that he gets up in the morning at the same time I do, and the first thing he does is he reads my Facebook page to see if I have a quote up there that gets me excited for the day. Then he tells me that he wants to meet up for coffee, and of course, we will.

And that's the whole point of it. It all goes back to gratitude and back to grace and compassion and making sure that when you're leaving your mark on the world, and whether we realize it or not, we are each leaving a mark on the world, that we're incorporating this into everything we do.

www.NextLevelMotivators.com

CHAPTER 8: Write a New Life Chapter

Your Past Doesn't Define Your Tomorrow

Right now, right where you are, in whatever mindset you find yourself in at this moment, give yourself permission to reject the pity party of life, the blame game and the victim state of being. It will never serve you, but it will prevent you from becoming who you were meant to be—the best version of you. So right where you are at this very minute, reject all feelings of how you have been mistreated, betrayed, injured, abused… all of it. This doesn't mean that all of that might be very true and accurate. What it means is that you are letting it out of your life, your head and your heart.

If you find yourself clinging to any of these feelings, please take out your journal and start writing all of it down. All of the details, all of the emotions, all of the injuries, abuse and betrayals and get them out of your mind and onto paper. Purge all of it and record it all.

Got it? Great. Now, cross a line, a single line, through all of it. Every detail, every hurt feeling, all of the pain, all of the fear, put a single line through all of it. Then, once it is all crossed out, write on a clean new page:

"I give all of the pain, fear and power of these circumstances back to you. You who have caused me harm are no longer permitted to harm me or haunt me—not in my thoughts, words, or actions. I am returning all of the pain and fear back to you. It doesn't serve me, so I will not keep it with me from this moment forward. I divorce all of it."

Visualize the pain and fear lifting from you. Feel the lightness of your spirit, in your head, in your heart, and visualize actually returning it all to those who have caused you harm. It's not necessary or helpful to return it with vindictiveness,

108

but as if peacefully returning a gift that isn't helpful or good for you.

Then claim the peaceful vessel that you are—the light-hearted newness that is within you, open and prepared to receive blessings, growth and joy. Embrace the curiosity of the new amazing gifts that are aligned for you now that you are no longer being held captive by your past.

Whether you're 15, 35, or 65 years old or even younger or older and everything in between, you still have a lot of chapters you have to write in this book that is your life. All that you've gone through have helped you to be more resilient, more insightful, wiser and more YOU. Each day, you are changing. You're growing and morphing into a new you based on your experiences, knowledge and your mindset. Sadly, for most people, they have very little to do with these changes—it's on autopilot, mapped out on whims, wishes, fear and pain without much if any deliberate intention taking place.

This is a tragic missed opportunity. Sit down with yourself and mindfully draft your next life chapter. You get to choose what it becomes but only if you put in the work. The battles, the agony and defeat have changed you. You can choose to let them destroy you or lift you up and make you greater. You write your next chapter—don't let whims or unintentional moods and fears write it for you. Most certainly, don't let another person, particularly someone who isn't healthy for you, write your chapter for you. It's your life; your story. Make it count!

Look Back

The chapter of my younger self when I was a beautiful young man, an exotic dancer, traveling the world, I was a womanizer, a seducer—I loved to be with women, and they loved to be with me. It was more intoxicating than anything else I ever experienced which is I why I never craved alcohol or drugs. This chapter was all about my relationships— whether they lasted hours, months or even when they lasted years and lead to marriage before crashing and burning. It was merely a chapter in my life not the whole book. I grew from these experiences—breaking other people's hearts, tearing my own heart open, disappointing others, disappointing myself. It was both intoxicating and tragic, and that was this particular chapter. It was shallow and messy, but it set the stage for the large, fulfilling, inspired life that I get to live now.

Of course, the fullness of storytelling is incremental and progressive. You build the arc in stages. From dancing, I decided to take my life more seriously by at least working with my clothes on, and I started bouncing in nightclubs and working in gyms. I even owned a tanning salon and a vitamin shop. Don't misunderstand me—while I wasn't taking my clothes off for money anymore, but my mindset remained the same. I was still a womanizer. I was still basking in the glow of the only thing about me that fed my self-esteem: my good looks. I just didn't want to take my clothes off on a stage anymore.

Making Sense of Insanity

In subsequent chapters of my life, I eventually learned to shed the addiction of the high that comes from being desired

110

by so many women and wanting them so badly in return, but it was gradual. You don't realize how things affect you until *you realize how things affect you*—until you experience something different and have an opportunity to look back.

A pivotal moment occurred when I was working with a guy who looked to be in his 50s, and he was still working as a stripper. He had a great body and all, and he danced well, but he was clearly on a downward slope in this game. He's not going to get better, more attractive or more seductive and soon everyone will be saying, "Hey, you look great—for your age." I knew that I didn't want to be that guy, and I wasn't getting younger either. I had to stop before continuing this gig became pathetic and tragic.

It wasn't a simple transition. My life was almost like being rock star I think. I imagine that it was similar to how a rock star feels partying on the stage with women throwing themselves at you after the show. The women just show up and there is crazy sex and orgies and all the things you'd imagine plus more. Then after I was in Playgirl magazine, it got crazier because now I'm autographing my own naked body in a centerfold, and I'm getting introduced everywhere all over the world. My ego shot up like a rocket, and that became a central part of my identity.

I needed to learn to find myself apart from this person who was steeped in this bizarre lifestyle. I knew it wouldn't last much longer, and that it was better for me to make the transition while I was still on top of my game than to leave as some over-the-hill, has-been who couldn't get gigs anymore. So, I took my proverbial baby steps towards that next chapter which is significantly more difficult than just going out and getting another job—updating my resume and looking at career options.

I was really caught up in all the glam and allure with the orgies and so many women just throwing themselves at me, but when I'd try to have a normal relationship, it was impossible to be normal. I barely knew what normal was because to me normal had become sleeping with a girl and her girlfriend. Monogamy and real intimacy felt so odd; it was almost impossible for me.

I'd meet a woman who was incredible, smart, beautiful, kind, had a good head on her shoulders with a good job, not a dancer… And I'd try to have a normal relationship. I'd get married and try to make it work. Towards the end of all the failed marriages, and after the last one, I said to myself, oh my gosh, I don't think I can ever be faithful.

I really believed that. I didn't think I'd ever be able to be faithful. I actually said a prayer to God. "God, please. I want to be faithful so badly. I've lost so many incredible women because this." I would honestly play with my girlfriend's best friends and you'd say, "Well, how would a girlfriend's best friend sleep with you? That's so wrong." It's not like that— it's still all about mindset.

I believed that I could get any woman I wanted, and I did. Think about Tiger Woods, when he believed he could beat anybody, he did. When he lost that mindset, he stopped winning. Michael Jordan would say the same thing. You have to be good at what you're doing, but it all starts with your mindset, and my mindset was on fire with this one skill I had developed as a womanizer. That's how I seduced women who otherwise wouldn't have considered sleeping with me.

TAKE ACTION: Write a New Life Chapter

When you are prepared to turn the page in your life and write a new chapter for yourself, I'll warn you that it's usually difficult to transition purposefully. It's easy to just go with the flow and let circumstances and whims carry you to the next phase in your life as you drift along with it, not making any deliberate, strategic changes to put your life on a course that is right for you. To write a new life chapter that is right for your purpose, right for your values, right for that vision in your mind of who the best version of you is meant to become won't be easy, but it's one of the most rewarding and empowering things that you will ever do in your life. Go ahead and start!

Journal: Begin in your journal, and literally outline your chapter here as if you were outlining a chapter in a book. This is a book of your life. Think of where you are in your life right now: your relationships, responsibilities, finances, goals, resources, etc. Now, think about the next step you're going to take to become the best version of you that you can be?

Start outlining this new chapter of your life. Going from where you are right now, what's next for you? Is it a new job, more education, a new relationship, activities with deeper purpose and meaning for you, beginning a new business, going on an adventure? What does this look like in outline form?

Writing: Next, go beyond the journal and outline, and actually begin the writing process for your new life chapter. Fill in your story with your dreams and goals. Map out how you will achieve these goals, and what it will look like, how it will feel. Don't be afraid to give us insight into what to expect in subsequent chapters. Remember, these are just words—

113

they can change. But, do be as detailed as possible to make this exercise as vivid and emotional as possible. Actually, write your next life's chapter.

CHAPTER 9: Confidence Attracts

I've spent a considerable amount of my life as a womanizer, seducing any woman I wanted—wherever and whenever I wanted. While I'm not proud of this trait that I've since completely removed from my personality, it taught me a few important skills that translate powerfully into other areas of life. One of the most beneficial of these skills has to do with confidence being the most attractive force in humanity. There is nothing as sexy, alluring, and impactful as true confidence that exudes from within. People who possess this can change the energy of a room when they enter, and they can translate this into charisma that's so strong it can capture attention. As a leader, it's how you attract followers. As a mentor, it's how you change minds. As an activist, it's how you change hearts.

Initially, I understood this as it pertained to sex. When you have your confidence intact when you approach a woman, you will win every single time. I could teach a guy who is not attractive at all how to walk into a room and attract women. If he walks in with massive confidence, dresses nice and carries himself well, he will get the attention of more women than he could ever imagine because very few people present themselves with true confidence.

Your self-esteem goes a long way in attracting people to you. And as I mentioned, this isn't just for attracting women; women can attract men with the same skill. All genders can attract whomever they choose similarly. It works for job interviews, in attracting business partners, in attracting followers to champion your cause and anything else. Your confidence, your self-esteem bleeds out of your pours, and others can see it and sense it. It's in your walk, your posture, your grooming, your eye contact and how you touch, speak with and interact with others. It's an energy others can feel when they are near you.

Authenticity

Confidence and its partner, self-esteem, must come from within, or people will sense that there's something phony going on—that you're trying too hard. Dressing "too sexy" or trying to be "too impressive" can also be turnoffs. It's about letting your inner-strength shine through. People will know that you're dressing how you dress, walking how you walk, saying what you say not to impress but because you don't care what anyone thinks. Your confidence is about being you and not being concerned with others' opinions. That's the big turn on.

It's not being arrogant or cocky; it's about being self-assured. Your self-esteem is driving you; you know what you want, who you are and you're confidently presenting that to the world.

That's not to say that the "fakers" don't reel in their catch, too. A beautiful woman or a great looking guy can lay on the charm and get what they want, but soon after, someone is going to see through that.

It's no secret that a beautiful woman doesn't have to try as hard as any average-looking woman. Any average guy is going to see a beautiful woman, and he doesn't care of she's intelligent, good-hearted, fun, etc. He's just going to look at her and think, "Oh, I have to have her. She's so sexy."

Then six months down the road, they made this relationship all about sex and soon he realizes that this girl has no personality, isn't kind or thoughtful, isn't particularly smart or anything else. But that didn't matter at the time. And then he just wants out when the sexiness has worn thin, and they need to face life together as a couple. He's standing there

117

wondering how it all went so wrong because he went for the wrong qualities for the wrong reasons.

Now hang on—no, I am not at all saying that all beautiful women are stupid, heartless, selfish… whatever. Many extremely beautiful women are brilliant, kind, wonderful people. What I was describing is a common issue guys, especially womanizers like I was, end up in when we don't check in on the personality of the women we want to take to bed. Our intentions are all shallow, so we attract "all shallow" to us. We only looked on the surface, and we ignored seeking out that inner glow of authentic confidence lighting up their eyes and searching for the goodness in their hearts. That's how many of us get into trouble in relationships.

So, while beauty might get you a temporary fix of what you think you're seeking, confidence—true, authentic confidence—will get you everything you want in life. It doesn't matter how good-looking you are or not, if you lead with confidence, you will confidently attract to you whatever you're after.

Faith Enters In

Of course, authentic confidence isn't shallow, right? It isn't formed from just wanting it, practicing it or forcing it to show up in your life. It's a process that comes from deep within and maybe it's not comprised of the same stuff for all people. For me, it had everything to do with my self-esteem, my faith in God and belief that my faith would lead my path.

Faith has remained a constant in my life, and it has been deeply connected to my sense of self-worth. Even back then, dancing and womanizing, my faith was a core component of

118

my identity. Yet, about five times per year, my faith really started to waiver, and that really shook me. I'd ask myself: who am I? What good am I? What do I stand for? Why would God love me? Do I have any worth?

When you don't know who you are or if you have any value, many things in life can control you—other people, addictions, sex, circumstances, anger, fear and so many other things. Yet when you learn who you are and what you stand for, you put your foot down on things that are out of alignment with your values, purpose and self-worth.

But when you're wavering in your sense of self, and you don't know who you are or what you stand for, you tend to do things that you normally wouldn't do. Then you start to make excuses for your actions, and you waver all over the place in your life. Your decisions become a sordid succession of compromises on what used to be your values, your integrity and your purpose. The old adage is true, "If you don't stand for something, you'll fall for anything." You'll find all of the excuses and rationalizations you'll need to justify anything, but deep down, you know you're lost and living outside of your authentic self.

Again, for me this had everything to do with my struggle with my faith. When that is out of focus, I became wildly out of focus, and I can only describe that feeling as horrible, lost, confused and even ashamed at times. A core reason my faith would waiver had to do with that issue of self-esteem and confidence. I knew who I wanted to be, but I didn't think that I could be that person or if I was good enough to be that person.

What changed was critically important, I went to my faith first! I didn't allow my self-doubt to deter me from my faith. I

119

went to my faith with my self-doubt and allowed my faith to change my heart.

The Confidence to Change

Let's be perfectly honest, change is really difficult. Real change, the kind that transforms your heart, mind, lifestyle, and values—that change can be terrifying. You're redefining yourself to yourself, and you think at some level that there's no way you'll succeed. However, not embarking on this inner journey is also terrifying. I had to become more terrified of not becoming the man I was supposed to be than the fear of failing at becoming him. My faith led me on that path, and it gave me the confidence I needed to stay the course. Even when I'd fail, even when I felt broken, even when I disappointed myself and others who mattered in my life, my faith in God, and really only that, gave me the confidence I needed to pick myself back up and keep becoming, blessed and unstoppable.

CHAPTER 10: Diving into Change

So, change is a process. And depending on the change you're facing, some change is exhilarating like getting married, graduating from college, getting a promotion, buying a home, or starting a new job. Other changes can be frightening or devastating such as the death of a loved one, losing a job, a divorce, etc. Plus, some people deal with change better than others allowing the process of change to go a little more smoothly, while others find all change, even positive change, to be extremely stressful. However, even to those who love change and embrace it with ease, it's still a process. When you face the process of change openly and purposefully, it opens a new world of opportunities for you. When you embrace change in this manner, you're not "going with the flow"—you're leading the process mindfully and with intention for a positive outcome.

This goes back to the concept of writing your own next chapter, and in diving into change, you're not allowing yourself the option to back out of it. You're not dipping your toe into unfamiliar waters to test it out. You've made a decision that you are going to dive all the way in to change because you must. You've likely made this decision because you've determined that change is critical to some important area of your life: your survival, your peace of mind, your personal and/or professional growth, for the betterment of your family, etc. If you've made the decision to dive into change, you've decided that the change is a "must" for you, and you are choosing to deliberately guide this course for the most positive outcome possible.

For me personally, diving into change in my life was triggered by two specific reasons: 1) honoring my faith, and 2) wanting to change course before I became a joke. My faith was pushing me to take my life in another direction—I wasn't fully the man that I knew I wanted to be in all areas of my life. For that to occur, I knew that my lifestyle needed a dramatic change. At some point, it is difficult feeling good about yourself, taking your clothes off with women yelling at you in a bar, etc. Plus, there were things about the company I was working for that didn't sit right with me. Then when I saw a 55-year-old exotic dancer, who was in good shape, I knew that I needed to get out before I became "that guy" who didn't know that his time was up. I was 30 at the time, and it was clear to me that my time for change was immediate.

And change was terrifying. I'm not going to lie to you about that. What other skills did I have? Was I good at anything else that I would get paid to do? What would my life look like once I stopped doing this? Who exactly was it that I wanted to become?

These were all questions that I knew I didn't have the answers for, but the first step was making the decision to dive into change even though the full trajectory of how it would all get sorted out was mostly unknown.

Nothing Is Meant to Stay the Same

While change is inevitable in life, deliberately deciding to make a change for yourself can seem scariest. You're afraid of making a huge mistake, and you'll only have yourself to blame if it doesn't work out, but you've decided that change is a "must" in your life for some critical reason, and here you are. In my case, I was living this mostly surreal life with good money and kind of this rock star energy when I went to work. I'm about to trade this in for being a working stiff, and how in the world was I going to earn the same kind of money that I was used to making without an education, no experience in any trade, no real work experience?

When I first stopped dancing, I had three jobs to try to earn the income I was used to. I opened a tanning salon, I also bounced at a nightclub at night, and I also worked at a GNC nutrition store. So, I had three jobs rotating back and forth to make the kind of money I needed for the lifestyle I desired. Plus, each of these jobs kept me in my comfort zone. From the tanning salon to the night club and the nutrition store, still surrounded by all of these good looking, healthy people. I was working out and getting my supplements for free.

Outwardly, it probably looked like I was living a cool life, but inwardly, I felt trapped. I was working all the time. I've never worked more hours in my life. And I felt I had no choice because I just didn't have any skills that would provide the income I thought I needed. In my head, I thought that I could never be anything more—my limiting beliefs were truly guiding my path.

And yes, I did own a tanning salon which I purchased because my dad invested in it for me. I had convinced him that this was going to be so great because I knew all of these strippers, bouncers and body builders who all use tanning salons, and this is going to be awesome! As it turned out, yes, I did know all of these people who I thought were friends, but really, they were just acquaintances. They would come in, and they all wanted something for free because they knew me. Okay, I had no experience in business at all, no management training, no business education, no mentors—I really had no idea how to run a profitable company. What's worse is that I'm the kind of person who will happily give others stuff for free. Of course, I think that when I do that, then they'll be loyal and come back and purchase packages, bring their friends in, etc. No, that didn't happen, and even their friends expected to get in for free. Once the free ride was over, they were gone, and of course, so was the business.

124

The worst part of all of it was that I let my dad down. That was the sting that just won't go away. Within one year, the tanning business folded, and my dad's investment was gone.

Needing a Mentor

So that was my attempt to change the chapter in my book, and maybe the most important thing that I learned was that I had no idea how to run a business. Yet, running a business seemed to be the only solution I could think of for a guy like me with few skills and no college to earn a decent living. So I learned that I need to be a better leader. I need to develop business management skills, and I needed to learn who was a friend and who was an acquaintance. It's fair to say that through this failure, I learned a whole lot from that chapter of change that helped me grow to become a better version of me.

Throughout our lives, we experience certain moments when we are best able to receive lessons and learn from them. We're not always in a state of mind to receive lessons. Maybe we're too busy or too distracted, but mostly it's when things are going too well for us that we skip over the lessons life brings to us. Usually, it's with pain and failure that we open up enough to receive the lessons presented to us. These are our most teachable moments.

I ended up learning about business management by watching others do it. Some did it really well, and I learned from that. Some did it horribly, and I learned what not to do from that. Probably the greatest mentor I had in business management was one of the guys who did it horribly. He took me under his wing and showed me how he did certain things well, and

125

that was helpful, but I already knew most of that by then. What I really learned from him was how not to treat employees. I heard what they all said about him when he would leave early so often or just didn't put in much work at all. His employees would all say, "That's so messed up. This guy hardly does any work." I vowed that I would never be that kind of manager. I would never be the person others would talk about saying that I didn't work hard or didn't have my employees' backs. When you show your employees that you value them, they work hard. When you treat your employees with compassion and lift them up, they stay with you.

This was in the early 90s, and we didn't have the benefit of YouTube or online video courses. My access to management materials was limited. I could have certainly read books on management (and by now I have read several), but because I still had it in my head that I wasn't very smart and I also didn't like to read because I thought that I just wasn't very good at it, I didn't explore that option early on. I just learned by observation—what to do and what NOT to do.

Today, I have several different kinds of mentors. Some are people I've met and know in person, and we participate in masterminds together and participate in coaching ourselves to become better coaches. Other mentors, I've never even met. I devour their online content, their YouTube videos, TEDx Talks, books, webinars and several other tools and resources they've developed. Mentors can appear nearly anywhere you look these days, just do your homework to make sure they are the mentors you want. Make sure that they are credible and that their message speaks to you and your goals in a meaningful way.

Redefining Moments

No matter your age, if you've reached adulthood, you've already written a few chapters in your life. You've already experienced change. Maybe you haven't been as mindful or strategic about writing those past chapters as you might moving forward, but they are written.

Here is a key point to remember as you proceed: Your past doesn't define you.

Other people might still remember you as you once were, but that's not your issue. You get to redefine yourself each blessed day you wake up in the morning. Just because some other people can't move beyond who you once were isn't something to concern yourself with. Keep moving forward anyway. Most will see the changes in you, and they'll catch up with you. Others won't, and they'll stay stuck in the past which is their loss not yours.

Too often we take the baggage from our past along with us, and we allow it to destroy our future. Don't do that. Leave the past in the past. Only take what you've learned from those experiences with you. Honor your past, but don't give it permission to haunt you today. It's over. Take what you've learned to become a better version of you—use the lessons from your past to propel you forward; don't let it hold you captive.

Most of us, hopefully, have learned in relationships that it's neither healthy nor productive to keep bringing up the past mistakes of your partner when you're arguing. If you haven't ever discussed or dealt with issues from the past between you both, that's a deeper problem that probably requires couples

127

counseling. What you're arguing about right now is in the moment, so stay there and work through it.

That's just an example; the real problem lies in the fact that we constantly do this to ourselves in our own minds all of the time. We're continuously allowing our past to haunt us, to cause us to second-guess our decisions, to interfere with our progress and potential, to support limiting beliefs that aren't true or that are no longer true, and we self-sabotage.

The most important thing that you can do to prevent self-sabotage as you are diving into change is to obsessively focus on who you are becoming. Dismiss your negative thoughts when they enter in, and focus on your purpose, your goals and your mindset. You do this by reading books that support your goals, watching videos, meditating, journaling and staying present.

It can be so hard to do. Those voices, thoughts and memories from our past keep playing out over and over sometimes. Until we learn to take their power away and quiet them, we have to use distraction and drown them out with more productive thoughts and messages. With enough practice, those memories that try to creep in won't make any sense anymore because you have become someone different. The contradiction between who you were and who you are now will become so great that your past will naturally lose its power to hurt you.

In my personal story, I had chapters in my life where I believed that I was stupid but very good looking. At first, I hadn't realized that I wasn't stupid at all or that being really good looking wasn't going to carry me everywhere in my life. In more recent chapters, I had to confront the truth of both of these limiting beliefs to write my subsequent chapters of

128

who I was becoming. If I wanted to be different, to fulfill my purpose that my faith was leading me towards, I had to prevent those former chapters in my life from taking over my thoughts for the future. I'm not stupid at all—I'm intelligent and highly capable, and I don't need to rely on my good looks to get what I want in life. Everything that I want now is in perfect alignment with my purpose in life.

Here I am today, a leader managing a business and owning another, and by anyone's standards, that takes some brains. That's of course scary for me if I let my past dictate to me who I am. I literally fight back against that daily. It's why I get up every single morning of my life and feed myself motivational videos, quotes, scripture and pray. One day at a time—limiting beliefs can be like an addiction, so every day, I wake up and combat them with positivity. That's how I succeed.

Daily Commitment

The daily commitment is critical to building new habits and creating lasting change. Every morning I wake up with my core purpose in mind. Every word of every morning, I stand grounded in the vision. I know who I am. I know that if I don't keep working on myself, my negative thoughts will have an opportunity to overcome and block my purpose. I will come into contact with someone that needs me that day, and my lack of focus, lack of self-esteem, lack of mindfulness won't let me be the best version of me for them, and that's not acceptable to me at this stage in my development.

If I can't be the person they need for me to be for them, that destroys me. So, either I could sit here and not become a better version of me and let everyone I've talked to down, or

129

I step up every day and work to be the best version of me that I have to offer. To me, there's nothing, nothing worse than letting people down. And because for me this is a faith-based purpose, I realized that if I don't keep working on myself, I let God down. That motivates me more strongly than anything else I can think of.

As long as I'm growing, taking steps—large steps or little steps, it doesn't matter—I feel as though I'm making a difference.

CHAPTER 11: Who Do You Want to Become?

You Are Who You Work to Become

Who you want to become can be a confusing or even frightening question for some people. It goes beyond asking someone "What do you want?" which is a common question within the personal development space. Who you want to become runs much deeper than determining your wants, because now we're asking you to describe and even wish upon your identity. Who are you now, what would you like to change about you, what are your values, are you aligned with those values, and how can you get better aligned with those values?

Answering these questions usually puts people in a space of uneasiness of not complete panic, and that's okay. Most things that are important are challenging. Again, that's why having a qualified coach or mentor to help guide you through the process is extremely helpful. Your coach will help ensure that you don't skirt around the difficult parts and that you don't miss important steps as you go through your journey of becoming your best version of you.

Many of my clients are individuals who are just stumbling into the thought process that maybe there could be something better for me. Maybe I could become somebody different or better. They enter into coaching often because they feel stuck somewhere in their life, and they're seeking assistance to breakthrough into the next chapter of their life in a purposeful way. That will require them to decide who they want to become.

Most people enter into the process asking the same common questions when they take their first steps on their inner journey. They ask things like, "Well, I'm okay with who I am, so I don't understand why I need to change. What's wrong with me?" or "Why do you want me to become someone I'm not?" No, no, no, that's not the point at all. The answers to these questions seem obvious to someone who is already deeply invested in a growth mindset, but to someone new to the process, they frequently resist the concept of examining and changing "who they are" at first.

Often we need to step back and examine all of the possibilities of who they could work to become, and why that would be important to them. We evaluate every area of their life to determine their strengths and areas that they might like to improve, and through this process, they begin to discover who they could work to become. The progress is awe-inspiring to be a part of. Literally, you get to guide and watch people decide that they must make different choices in their lives immediately to become this better version of themselves.

We're not seeking out perfection here, but for people to awaken to the idea that they get to choose who they are and what actions they are going to take to get into greater alignment with the identity of who they want to be. We say that "You are who you work to become" because the process begins with you already understanding that you are that person right now. You're just going to change habits, priorities and methods to uncover this person within you. You're not really changing yourself—you're setting your authentic self free.

Of course, it really gets down to the question—are you 100% happy with where you are in your life right now in all areas of your life? If your answer is yes, then great! You don't need me, and you can go out and do something else and not bother with a huge transformational process like the one I'm prepared to guide you through. However, if you would like to become a better version of you, if there is some area of your

133

life, or more, that you would like to improve, change and bring into greater alignment with your purpose, values, goals and vision, then, let's sit down and get to work. I can help you with that.

The Life Wheel

A central part of this first step in the process is the Life Wheel, which is a circular chart, like a pie chart, that addresses specific areas of life that we all have in common. Your family, finances, faith, and so forth are each listed there. Then you take your time thinking about each area of your life, circling a number from 1-10, with 10 meaning that you're doing the best in that area—it needs little to no improvement. One would mean that this area is horrible for you.

For instance, a ten in your finances has you with an 800+ credit score, great savings, retirement plan and income, and you're completely set in that area. Whereas a one in your finances might include a credit score in the 300s, you're deep in debt, maybe defaulted on some loans, maybe you're declaring bankruptcy and maybe you're income is so low you're on food stamps or have no current income, etc. A 10 in your relationships might have you happily married, you have a great relationship with your kids along with other family members and you have a strong support system of trusted friends whom you socialize with and you have each other's backs no matter what. Whereas, a one in relationships might be that you're going through a divorce, your children have stopped speaking to you and your friendships and support system are almost non-existent.

Often when we are only viewing life through our own lens, we can miss the true state of affairs with our assessment of

134

our life systems. This is another area where a coach or mentor can be immeasurably helpful. I can notice your hesitations and give you an opportunity to further examine your view of certain parts of your life. If you give your relationship a score of eight or higher, I might ask you if your partner, your wife, husband, boyfriend, girlfriend or whomever you're closest to, would score your relationship the same way?

This isn't about being right or wrong, but by really deeply examining these questions, you get the most realistic view to begin your journey. Only if you get extremely honest with yourself about where you are in these life areas can you begin to address them. Plus, it is a good idea to check in with your spouse or significant other because if you think that your finances are at a five, and they think that you're both at an eight, then it's time to have a discussion about how your perspectives are so different. Then you can honestly approach this issue for improvement. Making dramatic changes in life areas doesn't work so well if your spouse or significant other isn't on board with you on these changes, or worse—perhaps they will start working against you if they don't understand the value of what you're doing.

If you're single, and you say that your finances are at a five, then I'll ask you why you'd say that? Again, being completely transparent and honest here is key. Then we can set a plan to fix that, and we can fix it if you're willing to do the required work to become a better you. That might mean better budgeting and increasing your income along with other strategies like credit counseling, etc. Overall, what we're doing is assessing where you are in each area of your life so that you have a starting point on what you'd like to change. Then we can begin mapping out how to do that. Remember, at all times, these are still your goals, and there are no hard rules

135

here. If you examine your relationships, and you determine that they are at a five, but you're okay with that, and you don't want to change those now or ever, that's up to you. However, this intense examination allows you to make these decisions for yourself fully informed.

Adjusting Your Life

When we think about becoming the best you, examining and assessing each area of your life and determining where you would like to make improvements, it's best to think of these improvements as adjustments versus changing who you are completely. When you play a sport such as golf, tennis, basketball, etc.—once you have the game down, your coach usually doesn't work on changing everything about everything you do. The focus becomes on making small adjustment that drastically improve your game. So the old cliché is true: life is like golf. When you move your feet, twist your grip in a certain way, angle your shoulders, tilt your head… these small adjustments have an enormous impact on the success of your game.

That's precisely how the best life coaches approach guiding you on your journey to create a better version of you. It's not about reaching some level of perfection and changing everything about you. We guide you on a journey to make adjustments in areas of your life where you would like to experience improved success. This is why creating an accurate assessment in your life areas is so important—so that if you want to go from an eight to a ten, or a three to an eight, we can identify the exact adjustments that would be most helpful for your specific circumstances to achieve those goals. The adjustments that you would need to reach a ten in a certain area of your life will be completely different from another

136

person's needed adjustments. This is why coaching isn't on some broad, public platforms as a one-size-fits-all methodology. Each individual client must work one-on-one with their coach with complete honesty and transparency to get the most out of the process.

In determining the right adjustments for you, you really do need to decide who it is that you want to become. Some coaches recommend "finding an avatar" which could be a celebrity or some other public figure to emulate. Mentors can also be helpful as they focus on the business or financial areas of your life and help you process through their particular area of expertise to a degree of mastery. You may take classes on specific topics where you'd like to improve and even mental health, family or couples counseling if you feel that would be helpful. There are several different peripheral resources that combine exceptionally well with life coaching which will strengthen your ability to make adjustments in key areas of your life. All of this is aimed at your progression toward becoming whomever it is that you want to be.

A great example of this would be if you decided that a primary goal of yours was improved health and fitness. I'd recommend that you take a little time to research someone that emulates your fitness goals—perhaps it's someone that you can follow on YouTube. This doesn't have to be someone who is a symbol for all you want to be in life—just to emulate for your particular fitness goals at the moment. Then you can seek out others who can serve as role models for the other areas in life you'd like to improve like maybe someone like Dave Ramsey for finances or Phil Town for investments. These are just examples, of course—I'm not specifically recommending these guys to anyone. There are oceans of great experts that you can access online on nearly any topic, and you'll need to seek out the ones who best emulate who you'd like to become in that space.

When you start following them, focus on the key adjustments that they recommend that are in alignment with the changes you'd like to make in your life area. What are specific strategies that they do themselves or recommend for others that can help you to level-up and become the best version of you?

Attributes that might really speak to you about a particular expert could be that you love the way they talk about their subject, and their approach to it. They have a particular energy about them that works for you—maybe it's subtle or maybe it's loud, but it speaks to you. They aren't going to be your guru in all of your life goals. They are just going to help you strengthen the one area of your life where they are an expert. They'll influence you enough to make critical adjustments that will help you make the first steps toward the improvements that you'd like to see in that area of your life.

CHAPTER 12: Redemption—Action for Change

So far, we've talked about mindset and how shifting the words you use and the habits you develop can make a powerful impact on shifting how you perceive and respond to everything through an enhanced, positive mindset. We've talked about empowering yourself to make bold, deliberate and strategic changes in your life by truly digging in and evaluating key areas of your life and setting plans of action to get what you want out of those areas. We've also explored some specific activities to make lasting changes in your life by not just trying to change but by deciding that you must make these changes right now. All of this is truly inspirational and challenging work, so if you've come this far, and you've taken the steps outlined here, you are on a powerful path for personal growth and success!

However, nothing important in life is ever easy, and personal transformation certainly fits snuggly into that category. Not only is it challenging to develop consistency, to continuously re-evaluate your mindset to make the shifts needed throughout each day, but there are going to be times when your former mindset is going to charge in and betray you. You'll slip, and sometimes in big ways. I'm going to tell you right now that this is normal, healthy and to be expected. In fact, it's so normal and healthy that I'd be more concerned if I were your coach and this didn't happen to you.

What does it mean? Well, it's an opportunity for you to journey inside yourself a little deeper, with maybe a little more honesty and realism, and truly examine areas from your past that keep aligning you with setbacks and maybe even repeated failure. Almost all of us have parts of our past that we've tried to bury—maybe we're ashamed or embarrassed by something we've done or didn't do; maybe we've been terribly hurt and devastated by someone or something; maybe we made mistakes or others close to us did that had consequences that we wished we could undo. Whatever pain that we've allowed to hide away has been sending us messages over and over to be afraid, to feel unworthy, to feel ashamed, to feel incompetent, to feel… something that keeps us from enjoying sustained happiness and success.

And although you've made great progress so far (and if you've followed the steps laid out in the previous chapters, you truly have!), it's time to go back inside and release your attachment to the things that still keep holding you back. To forgive—yourself and others—and develop a renewed mindset of redemption is the next big step towards taking action for lasting change.

Here's what's great: you get to use the momentum you've already established in making changes in your life! By following the steps in previous chapters, you've had some success of re-framing your mindset, of examining what specific changes you want to make, and of taking action towards those changes. You've done more than just process by now—you've experienced change. Let that feeling help you propel through this next chapter. You now truly get to say that you're not the person you once were. You are who you are becoming, and that is your true superpower.

Releasing Guilt and Shame

While I've already explained that I spent the first half of my life believing that I was stupid, but that I found a sense of pride and belonging because girls thought I was good looking, it's now time for me to describe exactly how that played out in my life. I was a womanizer, an exotic dancer, and I was even featured in Playgirl Magazine as a centerfold model. I'm not at all ashamed of my past—it was a very important part of my life, but it's also not at all reflective of the man I am today. Yet there were consequences to this

141

mindset and lifestyle that I truly wished never happened. Unintentionally, I hurt people, and at no phase of my life have I ever been someone who didn't care if I hurt people or made them feel uncomfortable.

So I've had to go back and do some work with myself, find it in my heart to forgive myself, ask for forgiveness from others when it was appropriate and generally make peace with my past. If I hadn't, and before I did, no matter how much work I achieved in reframing my mindset, in becoming a better version of myself, the guilt of who I was had the power to drag me down at times and send me spiraling into a dark cavern of negativity, self-sabotage and even hopelessness.

One thing that I can promise you is that no matter how bad or messy or painful or pain-causing your life has been in the past, there is immense power in forgiveness of yourself and others. Redemption is possible. Every day you can choose to be a better version of you—something you'll do for yourself and your loved ones, but really, it's a gift that you can give to the world. It's a way that you can bless literally everyone who comes into contact with you as you approach life and challenges with a sense of hope, opportunity, positivity, action and gratitude.

Put the Past in the Past

On top of believing that I was stupid and struggling with massive issues of inferiority but at the same time, enjoying the attention of girls, I was also being molested by a man for a few years on and off. I honestly don't know what impact that had on me other than interrupting my innocence by the age of 10 or maybe younger. It did sexualize me at a young age, and I started thinking about sex and girls very differently. I

142

don't think that being molested made me a womanizer. I probably would have been a womanizer anyway, but I'm certain that it didn't help. It seems that most of the positive attention I received as a young person was sexual or at least physical in some way. This led to a much larger problem a little later.

So basically, when I was a teenager, about 16, 17, 18 years old, I was just starting to have sex with every girl in the world or so it seemed. At the same time, every other weekend, I stayed at my friend's house, and he had a sister who lived there. I was already a full-fledged womanizer, and beyond just trying to go to bed with every woman (or teen my age), women were little more than sexual interests to me, which eventually created a big issue in my friend's house with his sister. To describe my relationship with my friend's sister, I just sort of knew her. We weren't close; we didn't have our own relationship where we would spend time together or talk outside of my brief visits. However, she was a female just two years younger than me, and so I was "interested".

I would steal glances of her undressed whenever I could. I'd peek in as she was taking a shower, or I would look into her bedroom door. She used to run around the house in her underwear, and I'd take notice of her body. We never had sex or even kissed or anything like that, but she knew that I was looking at her and how I was looking at her. I didn't know she knew I don't think; I was a stupid teenager. I later learned that I made her feel very uncomfortable, and when I learned that, I felt awful! It's one thing for me to objectify nearly every female who walked in my path and want to try to sleep with them, but it's something completely different for me to learn that something I did hurt someone or made them feel badly.

Then, things took a sharp turn for the worse for me, but arguably it was probably better for her. One day we were wrestling on the ground, and I grabbed her breasts. Two weeks later, I was visited by the police and arrested. They asked me, "Did you ever touch your friend's sister when she asked you not to or when you weren't invited?"

I said, "I think I grabbed her boobs one time when we were just playing."

Bam! I got arrested for handling and fondling. I was 17 years old, and I was arrested for a sex crime. I did it. There was no defense for it, and I can hardly tell you how truly sorry I was and still am that something I did made another person feel that uncomfortable around me. And yes, it was more than just the one incident—it was all of it—but it took the one incident of me actually touching her breasts when she didn't invite or welcome it for her to finally be able to deal with the issue of this young guy coming to her house and making her feel so uncomfortable.

Honestly, that kind of helped me a little bit because I was terrified. I was terrified not only because of the consequences I was facing, but what weighed heaviest on my mind is that something I did, something I didn't even notice was a problem, made someone so uncomfortable that they pressed charges against me for it.

My lawyer asked me why I told the police that I had grabbed her breasts without permission? He couldn't understand why I would just outright admit to that. I honestly didn't understand what the problem was with it at the time. I knew that I would never rape anyone or anything like that—I knew who I was as a person, and I didn't think this was a big deal. I learned very quickly what a big deal it was, again, not because

144

of the consequences but because it made my friend's sister feel uncomfortable. What was just playful and fun or exciting to me was an extremely different experience for her.

How I made her feel bothered me for a very long time. My friend's sister and I are friends now, and we've discussed what happened openly. I apologized and told her that I would never mean to do anything to hurt her, and I had no idea how what I was doing affected her. She explained that she understood that, but it all made her feel uncomfortable.

I've mentioned a few times that what bothered me most wasn't the consequences I had to face, but I want to frame that in its proper perspective because the consequences were a little frightening. Of course, I was questioned by police, arrested and went to court to face sexual offender charges. I was 17 when the incident occurred, but I was 18 when I was charged. My sentence included community service hours and probation, but the most difficult thing was the court-ordered counseling.

While counseling probably doesn't seem so bad, this was group counseling for sexual offenders, and I'm sitting in a room and sharing my story with others who are sharing their stories, most of whom were rapists, serial child molesters and guys addicted to child porn. And there I was trying to explain that I was just looked at her and touched her breasts. To be honest, the whole experience was a wakeup call, and it got me to understand how bad this all really was and could be. It caused me to be a lot more cautious and aware of how others felt even if I thought something was just playful or exciting.

I had to attend these counseling sessions for about six months, and they wouldn't let me leave unless I admitted to being a pedophile. It crushed me. That wasn't true—that's

145

not who I am. They made me lie about who I was just to get out of the counseling. So eventually, after so much time spent protesting against this false label, I lied, and I admitted to being someone I am not and have never been.

This didn't change everything for me, of course. While I was more cautious and much more aware of others' feelings, I was still sleeping with all kinds of girls—I was still a womanizer. In fact, my lifestyle took a sharp turn into a situation where it was common for me to have women, literally, throwing themselves at me. I became an exotic dancer, capitalizing on my looks and charm, and I was really good at it. My career had me traveling the world, and it was amazing. I was a Playgirl centerfold model—women asked me to autograph their magazines—it was wild! The money was great! The orgies were a thing, and I soaked it all in. One thing I always prided myself on, though, was that I never went out and "partied"—that was never my scene. When everyone around me was lit, that's where I drew the line that I wouldn't cross.

Forgiveness is Freedom

Here's the moral to that whole story. It's too easy for me to feel horrible about what I did and the consequences that I faced. The shame of how I made my friend's sister feel by what I did, the humiliation that I endured as a consequence, the fear of what others thought of me when they found out, the guilt of what I thought of myself then and now whenever I dare to think about this time of my life—it's all overwhelming.

Most of us have moments in our past that we hold onto in a powerfully negative space. Forgiving ourselves doesn't mean that we believe whatever wrong that occurred is okay now. What it does mean is that you give yourself permission to no longer allow that wrong to hold you under in guilt and shame. You're allowed to break free from your past and define, embrace and become a new you—every day of your life!

It literally doesn't matter what you've done in your past—if your family won't speak to you, if you're in prison, if you've lost your job and are struggling to survive—no matter what, you are worth forgiving yourself. In fact, you owe it to yourself and everyone around you to forgive yourself, because only when you do that, are you capable of true, lasting transformation. Otherwise, your past will continue to haunt you, continue to insist that you remain the person you always were and pull you back each time you take a few steps forward. Forgiveness is your freedom, and I invite you to break free!

Overcoming Self-destruction

The sad part about real human growth is that most often growth is birthed from a place of destruction. I wish we could grow without having to be destroyed, and maybe some people can. Most typically, however, we find ourselves in utter desperation and decide that we must make massive changes right now, or we'll likely be doomed to a life of despair.

And while many of us do end up in a massive pile of self-destruction before we decide to rebuild ourselves. The details of what destroy us are incredibly diverse. For me, it had everything to do with experiencing the death throes of my fifth failed marriage.

To catch you up a little on life events, I had already blown through four marriages, completed a long and lucrative career as an exotic dancer, decided to open my own business (with my dad's money) and failed at that, then moved on to working in the fitness and supplements industries, respectively. Eventually, I decided to make my first round of serious life-changes, and I embarked on a career of public speaking and life coaching. This pivot wasn't accidental. I often found myself serving as a life coach to several of my clients at the gym, except that I wasn't charging for it, and I really didn't have a formal method involved with it. I loved it, though, and I really felt like it was giving me a greater purpose, so I started to take it very seriously. I joined Toastmasters, and I voraciously studied everything I could get my hands on to really help others.

Then, here comes the fifth marriage. Imagine loving someone more than you have ever love anyone in the world. Here you are, having finally found the woman that you think is the most empowering, incredible, stunning, every powerful word you can think of, and you have the biggest dreams and ambitions together. Not just marriage, but you would be the power couple of power couples, incredibly successful, owning our own company, speaking all over the world—we had it all: faith, family, health, fitness, success... This is what I saw in us.

In her, I saw this powerful, confident woman—she spoke differently, carried herself differently, and I was in love! We did make a truly amazing team, at first. Then, the woman that I loved more than anybody in the world was broken, and those broken bits eventually shattered off shards of glass that she used as weapons. She took all of her pain and insecurities and she wielded them straight at me with all the venom she

148

had hitting at all the weak points she knew about me to make sure each blow counted.

Then, with all of my pain and insecurities, I just exposed more wounds, and buried those shards of glass in deeper because of course I felt that I deserved it. That began a treacherous dance between two broken, destructive people who thought they had it all together. However, what they forgot to include in their foundation was forgiveness, healing, and redemption.

Today, we're incredibly close friends—well past the divorce. But at the height of things, she broke me more completely than I've ever been broken my life. It was, by far, the most incredible and the worst relationship I've ever had, and it's highly likely that I would have not been able to reach the level of healing that I have had it not been for that experience.

It brought me to a place of brokenness where I eventually realized that everything she put me through made me recognize that I am actually worth something. I'm worth living; I'm worth saving; I'm worth being here for others. But I had to find that in myself, and I had to dig so deep and confront those dark parts of my past to find a light of redemption. Am I just a high school dropout? Am I just a womanizer? Am I just a loser? Am I just...? Where's my self-worth? Where do I go from here? Where do I go from this broken man with these big, incredible dreams that have just been pulverized to nothing, and I mean nothing! I'm just this old ex-stripper that was in Playgirl that amounted to nothing. My looks aren't as good as they used to be which is all I thought I ever really had going for me. So, what in the hell am I?

I was faced with two choices: I give up, or I push through the pain and become the man I'm supposed to be. Who was I if I wasn't the man who empowered people over the last few years? Is everything that I've gone through meaningless?

The Face of Despair

Being broken and dwelling in despair doesn't look the same on everyone. It comes with different wardrobes, and some people are better at it and/or take more effort in hiding their despair than others. However, I assure you that the person who is in it knows when they're in it. You feel your sense of hope that things will ever get better slipping away. You lose your will to keep fighting and pushing through to get to a better place. You're truly prepared to give up and walk away from everything and everyone or worse.

The point of recognizing the face of despair is not so that you can prolong it and live in it, but it's specifically the opposite. Once you recognize it, quickly do the work to get out of it, and ask for help! Most of us have been there, to varying degrees, so we know the score. As much as you think everyone is going to judge you or shame you—that's honestly the last thing kind, healthy people will ever do. Since most of us have been there, we know the shortcuts out, so please ask for a little help. We really can help, especially when you think that we can't.

If you're there right now, please reach out. If you're convinced that you have to go through it alone, then my best advice is to begin with prayer and gratitude. Find even the smallest things you're grateful for: sunsets, the smell of fresh cut grass, puppy whiskers tickling your nose… then move to bigger things, like maybe your health, a relationship that's

150

special to you—write them down and really visualize. Then I turn to prayer, and I ask God for guidance, strength and His will to be revealed.

My darkest moment was driving on the Skyway Bridge, and thoughts of driving off of the bridge raced through my mind. I didn't do anything; there was no attempt, but the desire to just end all of the pain immediately was absolutely present in my mind. I turned to God. I promised, promised, promised myself that I would not have another failed marriage—my fifth marriage—but this one was literally killing me.

What became clear in that moment was that I didn't really know who I was after all—I gave my identity away to someone else, someone I love. All I really knew was how I thought I was supposed to be in a marriage. I was brought up to get married and put the other person first. I thought that when you put the other person first, everything will be okay because our Christian values would take care of the rest. I was also taught to humble myself and to make sure my wife is the most important person in my life and to treat her like a queen.

What happens in that scenario when you're in a relationship with someone who is broken is that all that value you've poured into them comes out in resentment and venom aimed back at you. You're waiting to be filled up like you filled them up, but it turns on you until you've given all you have to give, and there's nothing left for you anymore. I became cold, empty and pained. I gave up all of my self-worth, and I held nothing for myself.

That's a dire mistake in any relationship. I know that now. Self-love is critical, self-care is critical, self-worth is critical—you can't be someone's rock if you're crumbling at their feet because they're falling apart and are content to take you down with them.

I'm not the person I was back in my fifth marriage. I've become a stronger, empowered, humble, and loving man who truly knows his self-worth and what he wants. I'm not settling for anything less than that same sense of self-worth, strength and humbleness in a partner so that we can lift each other up not tear each other down.

Know Yourself

"If you don't stand for something, you'll fall for anything."

I believe in myself. I believe in my self-worth. I now know with my full heart what I'm created for, and I know my purpose. Let me tell you something, when you know your purpose, things drastically change in your life; I mean, drastic. I can't emphasize that enough. That's so important to me, because when you become beat down like I had been for so long, by the end of that fifth relationship, I would honestly say I was a shell of the man that I was when I walked into it, and I'm not exaggerating. I wasn't recognizable in the end. My body was totally out of shape. I had just let myself go. I didn't even want to go to the gym. I didn't even want to work out because I didn't believe in myself. I was that low. I'd think: *Why? Why do anything if I can't make my wife happy? Why even be here if I'm so worthless? Why do I bother to do anything?*

When you lose your sense of self-worth, and there are so many people out there who don't believe in themselves anymore, you go down a spiraling hole of despair and self-loathing. You can't imagine anyone thinking anything you do is of any value. Taking care of yourself—why? Performing

152

well in your job—why? Showing concern for other people you love—why? Everyone else would be better at it than you anyway.

Your mindset will truly determine your destiny, the course of your life and whether you are successful or not, no matter how you define success. A negative mindset like the one described above will cause you to crash, absolutely. A positive mindset will cause you to soar, absolutely. Remember: *whether you think you can or you can't, you're right!*

I'm very thankful that I didn't get into the "party scene" to deal with my emotions—never have. So addiction was never a problem for me, but I think I can understand the allure of numbing your pain like that. I used to say, "I can't imagine how could someone kill themselves? How could they do that?" Well, at the end of that relationship, I understood how that was possible. If it wasn't for my faith in God, if I didn't have a faith in God, I would have definitely been close to ending it all. If I had been drunk or high, I could see how suicide would have been possible. I really do, because I wanted everything to end, and I didn't want to go through this agony of being a loser in every area of my life.

You see, I didn't realize yet that I had the power to shift all of that with just my mindset. I had done a lot—a whole lot—of personal development work on myself, but I hadn't dug deep enough to really heal and forgive until I truly broke.

Take Action for Change

This all comes down to taking decisive action for change in your life. When you release guilt and shame, act on the knowledge that forgiveness is freedom, overcome your self-

153

destructive moments, recognize the face of despair, then ultimately you will find redemption and take action for change—you are on the road to profound healing and sustained transformation in your life. It's a life-long journey with peaks and valleys all along the way, but the more practice and guidance you get, the less time you find yourself in those valleys and the more time you get to spend on the peaks!

It's the same as anything else in life—the more you put into it, the more you'll get out of it. Thus, the more action you take towards positive change, the more positive change you'll get as a result. It's all about taking action. Mindset is only half of the battle though it's a very important one. You still have to put in the work.

One great way to keep the momentum going in taking action in your own life is to help others in some meaningful way. Perhaps it's being an accountability partner. Maybe you're mentoring at-risk youth or coaching a youth sports team. Perhaps you can lead a group of volunteers to help the in the community such as doing chores for seniors once a week or organizing collections of clothes and food donations for families in need. Each time you reach out beyond yourself to be a light and support for others, you're doing the work needed to be a better version of you. Each time you reach out to share your knowledge and your gifts with positivity, love and compassion, you're taking real action that's lighting up the world with the goodness it so desperately craves.

As for me, by helping other people grow, through coaching and mentoring, I often see how their situation reminds me of a time in my life and how I overcame a similar scenario, and I share with them what I needed to do, and where taking that action brought me further in my path to transformation.

154

Those moments remind me that I never want to settle, and that I need to keep taking action to move forward on my journey. I never want to go back to that place where everything was bleak and hopeless, so I must put in the work and be mindful of the messages I allow to sit in my head.

In 12-step programs, you sponsor people because you love the results of the actions you took to get out and to get to where you are now, and now you can help someone else go through those same positive actions. All the while, you're still growing as a person by helping someone else. It's really important to not get so stuck in your own world that you lose connection with others through your journey. Reach out to others, and grow that way, too.

Goals in Action

Setting goals is a serious step in taking action, or you could be taking all the action in the world while not actually achieving anything. If you don't know where you're going, it's almost impossible to get there, and you wouldn't know you've arrived even if you were already there. You need goals to set your course, to keep you motivated and to give you momentum and excitement to achieve them.

It's interesting when I talk to my clients about goals. If they say they don't have any, I have an idea where they're going to be a year from now—exactly in the same spot. I don't care if these are fitness goals, career goals, relationship goals, etc. It's all the same—goals set you on the course for your actions.

Then action takes its cue, and real, lasting change only occurs when you take action towards your goals every day, and I mean every day. To clarify, an action can be a step of

155

something tiny; it doesn't have to be earth-shattering. But, if you don't take the action step to complete your goals, they'll always be the same goals you had last year and the same ones for this year. Then you look back, and you wonder why you're not successful because your goals are just wishes and dreams until you start taking consistent action towards them.

CHAPTER 13: My Kids Make Me a Better Man

Bryson and Bella are two of the very most important people I have ever been blessed to meet in my entire life. I don't have any biological children of my own, but these two kids came into my life from different paths; they've changed my life for the better, and I am so grateful every day to be a part of their lives. This chapter is dedicated to these kids. Bryson is now 20, and Bella is eight years old at the moment of writing this chapter, and they are two extraordinary people who have lifted and lit up my whole world.

My Son, Bryson

A note to Bryson: *Bryson, when you came into my life, you were a small child, and you have grown into an amazing young man. Thank you for giving me a chance to be your father. Thank you for letting me be a part of your life. I am so proud of you, and you continue to amaze me all of the time with your quick wit, talent and the unique way that you see the world. Because of you, I see the world differently with its many challenges but also its vast opportunities. I pray that God allows those opportunities to continue to unfold for you throughout your life. We are blessed and unstoppable!*

I met Bryson when he was about six years old. I married his mom, which technically makes him my stepson, but I've always just thought of him as my son. Bryson's dad wasn't really in the picture, which was complicated for me, because I wanted Bryson to have a relationship with his biological father. Bryson is such an incredible person, and he deserves all of the love and support in the world. I don't know why his father didn't make an effort to be in his life, but at the beginning, I'd encourage Bryson to call him just to keep a relationship going. I'd have to explain to Bryson that I didn't know why his father didn't come to see him, and that was really difficult. There was a short time that Bryson's mom and

I were not communicating well, and she wouldn't permit me to see Bryson for a while, and that broke my heart. So I have no idea why Bryson's father wasn't around.

Bryson had the option of calling me anything he wanted when his mother and I got married, but after a short while, he chose to call me "Dad" because he didn't really know that other guy. When I look back on my whole relationship with Bryson, I think he has done more for me than I have ever done for him. I always wanted to be a dad, but I just wasn't able to have children of my own. Bryson is that for me—I love him as any parent loves their child; I love him unconditionally, and I am so honored that he includes me in his life.

With Bryson, not only did I have a son, but I got really lucky because he's truly an outstanding person and always has been. He's great at sports, has a great personality, is incredibly smart and very humble. All parents hope that their kids have all of these qualities, and I can say with absolute confidence that Bryson does have all of these qualities. His mom, of course, had a lot to do with that. She raised a young man with a giant spirit, and the world is blessed because he's here.

Before I met Bryson's mom and, of course, Bryson, I thought that I'd never be a dad to anyone. I did a lot of steroids early in my life and that creates reproduction problems, so I knew that I wasn't biologically able to have children of my own. It was a sad realization because I always thought that I'd be a dad, but I came to terms with it quickly. Then the opportunity came for me to be a dad to this little boy and to stay in his life for the rest of our lives, and I never knew that my heart could feel so full.

I've been in so many relationships that have failed but being someone's dad—that's not something that you can let fail. I had a chance to be there for a kid whom I love completely, and I was determined to not let him or us down with this responsibility. I might fail at many things throughout my life, but I was committed to being successful with this; nothing could be more important. The first part of my life was all about just doing things for myself and maybe pleasing other people, but this relationship with my son was something completely different. Now, I wanted to be a good example for him. I wanted to be someone different, someone he could look up to and be proud of. Of all the many things I've messed up in my life, I was committed to this not being one of them.

When Bryson's mom and I were getting a divorce after a five-year relationship, I remember very clearly talking to him about it. I said to him, "Hey, listen. I will always be here for you, no matter what, you know? Your mom and I didn't work out, but that doesn't mean that I won't still be your dad. I'll still be there for you, to pick you up or whatever you need."

That meant everything to me—I just wanted to be there for him and for him to know that he could count on me no matter what. And it was always about the little things, the memories and the time spent together. I remember all three of us lying in bed, watching a football game together, cheering, yelling, jumping on the bed and the little moments laughing together, discovering something together and just enjoying being together. The magic is always in the little things, never the big things.

Building trust with a kid is a profound experience. Especially as they start getting older because you don't think they're listening to you at all. Still, you keep talking, keep guiding,

160

keep offering advice, etc. Then you look up, and they're doing the opposite of what you had just advised, and you see what they're doing isn't working. They see that what they're doing isn't working. Then you talk to them and advise them again, hoping this time it might sink in; then, eventually they apply your advice, and it works out.

A great example of this between Bryson and me was when he was young, about eight years old, playing football. I'd take him to football practice, and I've followed football my whole life—I know this sport really well. I remember on a few occasions saying to him, "Bryse, you're not listening to me. I'm telling you, if you just do this, do this, do that… you'll be fine. You'll get the tackle or whatever it is." I'd keep telling him and telling him, but he wouldn't listen. Then in one of the games, he was lined up, and I saw him make the moves I recommended. Then I told him to go the other way, and he did it exactly the way I told him. He sacked that guy!

Okay, that was nice, but what made it awesome was that after the game, he ran up to me, and he said, "Dad, I told you I was listening to you." For me, it wasn't about him listening to me and being obedient or something—I was privileged that he trusted me enough to actually follow my advice. That was huge, and to this day, I'm honored to have that type of relationship with him. The most important thing to me was to be a person that he could trust, to be someone that he could look up to, to be someone who would always be there for him, and that's everything I still aspire to be for Bryson.

Black and White

Racial differences are not something that I have spent much time thinking about throughout most of my life which has a lot to do with me being a white guy and the luxury that comes with that. However, Bryson is black, and we are living in a time where racism is prevalent and potentially dangerous, so I am vigilant, and I do worry about my son and his safety in a way that I never realized that I would. Occasionally, someone will look at my white skin and assume that it's okay to make a racist statement to me, and I'm floored! I correct them, of course. I don't know why so many are surprised that there are mixed-race families, but Bryson and I are a mixed-race family. Fortunately, not all misunderstandings about our relationship are hurtful and dangerous—sometimes, they're funny.

One example was a time when we were at a 7-Eleven, and this is the same spot I go every day on my way to work. On this particular day, Bryson, who was about nine years old at the time, was coming to work with me. We saw the same Black lady there that I see daily, working behind the counter. Bryson is at the counter, and the lady says, "Can I help you, young man?"

He said, "Yeah, my dad is gonna pay for this."

"Where's your dad?" she asked.

"That's my dad right there," he said pointing to me as I was standing right next to him.

"Oh, stop it," she said.

"What, because I'm Black?" Bryson asked.

That was really funny—she saw me nearly every single day, and she was obviously surprised by the fact that I have a son, and he is Black. Bryson was a young kid at the time, and he thought it was funny; we laughed about it.

162

It's been an interesting dynamic because if Bryson's biological father was in the picture, we might have a different relationship. I'd step back, out of respect for his blood relative, and I wouldn't be "Dad," I'd be "stepdad". Bryson has asked me not to include his father in things because he said that he doesn't know him. I wanted to invite Bryson's father to his graduation, but Bryson said, "Please don't do that, please. I'll be so mad." So I didn't.

However, now that Bryson is older, and our society is still battling racism in large and sometimes dangerous ways, we've shifted into having more specific discussions about things that I believe you only have with Black young people. We talked about what to do and what to say if he is ever pulled over by the police. I could just see Bryson with his fiends being rude to a police officer if they felt that they were being treated unfairly. There's a phrase that Black Lives Matter demonstrators have been using, "Hands up; don't shoot," to describe what parents are instructing their Black children to do if they ever encounter police officers.

A while back, Bryson and I were talking, and he said that he understood rioting and vandalizing buildings during protests and why people are doing that. I was so alarmed, and not only did I try to correct his thinking, but I spoke with his mother, truly panicked, to make sure that she had the same conversation with him. She assured me that Bryson was just trying to get a rise out of me—that he would never think or do anything like that. We raised him better than that.

She was right, of course. Bryson is a great young man with a level-head. It's just so scary to think about the risk young Black men take in our society just for being young Black men.

I feel that I can understand more issues within the Black culture than I would be able to if I wasn't a part of his life. I see what is happening with everything from systemic racism to police brutality and killings, and I'm affected by it far more deeply than I would be if Bryson wasn't my son. I'll be honest with you, if I had a white son who was getting pulled over by the police, it wouldn't cross my mind that he would be hurt by them. Having a Black son, it's an enormous and real fear, and I know that how my son decides to respond if ever in one of these situations will make all the difference for him.

I absolutely believe that most police are heroes, putting their lives at risk every day, protecting our community to the best of their ability. However, the senseless fatalities of Black men in America by white police officers is a chilling trend that can't be overlooked, and I believe all parents of Black children are living in a state of fear for their kids. I really do try to understand both sides, but there comes a point when you must be honest with yourself and realize that there's no right side to someone in a position of authority, like a police officer, killing someone when there were other options, non-fatal options.

Of course, this runs deeper in our culture than just the police, although those instances are the ones capturing all the headlines. I operate a gym and some of the members there I've known for a very long time—some I talk to every day. One guy was in my office talking to me and as he was talking, he blurts out, "I'm so tired of this damn negro [stuff], you know what I mean"?

This man had never met my son, but regardless, he seemed to think that because I am white that I clearly must agree with him. I was trying not to spout off with a knee-jerk reaction, so I simply explained that I didn't see it that way at all. I was

164

seething inside because to me, it felt like he was insulting my son, my son's race and who my son was as a person.

Then on some other occasion, another guy walks over to me and starts talking about a mixed-race couple at the gym who were black and white. He said, "You see that couple out there? The young couple with the black guy and a white girl? You believe that [stuff]"?

I looked over, and I said, "Why, what's up? Get out if you're going to be racist." I knew what he was trying to say, but I was hoping he'd take the hint and drop the topic.

Instead, he continued, "There's that fine ass girl with that [n-word]."

I looked at him, and I said, "Don't say that. Don't use that word here."

He said, "What? I'm just being real. Like, she can't find a white guy is just killing me."

So, I repeated myself, "Please don't use that word in my office, please."

He said, "I'm not trying to be mean, but you know what I mean, man; you know what I mean."

I said, "No, I don't know what you mean."

Most people don't know that my son is black, but honestly, that shouldn't matter. Why do people think it's okay to speak freely about their obvious racism and prejudice? How did we get to a point in our society that because I have white skin, someone automatically assumes that I'm going to support,

165

agree with or allow their racist comments to go unchecked? It crushes me. I understand that in most cases their parents raised them to think this is okay, but it's not okay. At some point, we're all responsible for our own actions, and perpetuating racism is not okay, ever, under any circumstances. There is enough cultural competency in our schools and corporate environments and even in some cases through media, that people should have learned.

I've even tried to ask people who make racist comments why they do it. "Why do you have such a problem with black people?" I asked.

He said, "Bro, so I was in the Vietnam War, and I gave one a chance. I gave one a chance. We were in a bunker together, bro, and I thought we were friends. He turned his back on me, and I'll never trust one of those [n-word] ever.

I looked at him, and I said, "Bro, we'll be praying for you. So, you're telling me that no white person has ever turned their back on you or done you wrong?"

"Well, I gave them one chance. That's all I gave them," he said.

At some point, I realized that the problem was bigger than me, and that there wasn't anything I could say to change these hearts.

From the Heart

When Bryson was leaving for college, headed on a plane to go to Whittenburg in Ohio where he had a scholarship, he wrote a letter to me. He asked me to open it after he left, and

166

I have it framed in my bedroom. He got straight to the point, and he said, "Dad, thanks for everything you've done for me. I've learned so much…"

I would text Bryson every day, maybe three of four texts every day, especially over the past 5 years. I'd say things to him like, "So, be a man of your word." I would text him that every day for about a week. The next week, I would text him something else, and I might explain why it's important to "be different"—to be willing to stand out. I explained to him, "There's going to be times in your life that you're going to have to step out and be different. Your friends are going to walk that way. You're going to have to walk the other way." I also explained to him why I use the words, *Blessed and Unstoppable* and what it means to me. I encouraged him to find something that motivates him.

I often send Bryson these uplifting messages and remind him that faith in God is important, especially because there are going to be times when there's no one else around, and your faith will be the most important thing in the world to you at those moments.

And from all of this, my son wrote me a letter. In it he also said, "I'm so glad that you're in my life because I never would have known how to throw a football or catch a football or run down the sideline and do the things I did in my sports. A lot of it had to do with you, and I appreciate that." And then he said, "Thank you for helping me understand that I need to put God first in my life…" He melted my heart. I'm a sensitive guy, and that melted me.

One of the things that meant so much to me in his letter is that he understood that the best parts of life are made up of all the little things. He mentioned learning to throw and catch

167

a football, and that was a very special thing between us. When he was about six years old, I would take him to elementary school, and we would leave a half hour early so that I could teach him how to throw the football. I'd parked the car, and we'd get out on the back streets over by the elementary school just throwing the ball back and forth. That's when I first taught him how to throw a football. And we did that all through his elementary school days, leaving a half hour early each day. Then, the older he'd get, we'd do more like pretending he was in a game, running down the sideline. Moments like that we will never forget together. I live close to where we played, and when we pass by that spot together, we remember and talk about it. The best parts of life are in the little things, and he seems to really understand and cherish that, which makes me so proud.

That Bryson wrote that letter to me and what he wrote in that letter means so much to me that it's a little difficult to express. He wasn't just thanking me—he was validating all that I have tried to be for him. When I was young, I wanted to be just like my dad. He was someone I never wanted to disappoint, because I think of him as being an incredible man, someone I always looked up to. I wanted to be just like him because everyone loved him, and I always admired his faith in God, too. My deepest hope is to be that person in Bryson's life—to be the man that he looks up to, someone he admires because he sees something in me that's good, honest and worthy.

My desire to be, not just a good dad, but a man worthy of having a young man look up to me, pushed me harder to be a better person—to be more like my own dad and to be different. So, quite a bit of what has driven me to make positive changes in my life had to do with wanting to be the best dad I could for Bryson.

My Daughter's Name Is Bella

Her name is Arabella, but she goes by Bella. I met her when she was one year old, and she is the most special little girl in my whole life. I met Bella's mom before Bella was born when she joined the gym that I run. At the time, Bella's mom was pregnant and in another relationship, but that didn't work out. We became close about a year after she had her baby Bella. Initially, there was some real tension between Bella's dad and me—I was trying to be incredibly supportive of Bella's relationship with her biological dad and remind her that I'm just here, but that's your daddy over there. With young children, it's difficult for them to understand the various roles of the people in their lives, but how that confusion plays out can be devastating to the people who love them.

There was a particular moment in an airport where Bella and her mom are returning from visiting family, and I'm there waiting to pick up Bella's mom while Bella's dad is also there waiting to pick up Bella. Well, as soon as Bella sees me, she starts running to me and not her dad. I'll admit, that made me insanely happy, but I quickly directed Bella over to her dad, so she'd start running that way.

It's difficult because with Bryson, my son, his biological dad wasn't around, so we have a certain relationship where he calls me "dad" and sees me as his dad. With Bella, it's a little different. I love her as though she were my own child, but she has a dad who is active in her life and who loves her very much, and I honor that. Bella's dad does not like me, and honestly, I can understand that. I have a close bond with his daughter that is very much like a father/daughter bond, and he's concerned that I'm going to mean more to Bella than he does. I don't want that to happen, but no matter what, I love Bella, and I will always be there for her.

Jealousy hurts, and people become jealous because they are in pain, and they wished that things were better for them. I wished that there was an easier way to explain to Bella's father that my bond with Bella wasn't a threat to him—it just meant that his daughter had an extra dose of love, support and prayers; I wasn't trying to replace anyone—I was just adding to the list of the many people who loved Bella.

Bella was one year old when I met her, and she was the cutest thing I'd ever seen in my life. God works in mysterious ways. I ended up having a little girl and a little boy in my life. It wasn't the way I expected it, but it was perfect for me. Plus, Bryson and Bella even acted like brother and sister when they were together, which was the best thing I could have ever hoped for with them.

Bella has two other brothers, Keelan and Trent, but they were much older when I came into their lives. Keelan was an adult, and Trent was 12 with no interest in having a stepfather. With Bella, we have cleared up our roles and relationship—I'm the stepdad, and she has her dad and mom. Although I had been divorced from Bella's mom (more on that in the next chapter), she has always wanted me to remain in Bella's life, and I'm immeasurably grateful because that spirited, brilliant, creative little girl means the world to me.

In modern terminology, we have what is referred to as a "blended family", but to me, it's just my life. It's a little bit messy and confusing at times, and it's not like we have clear-cut rules to what families need to look like, and I for one am incredibly happy about that! These people are my family and my heart. This little girl that came into my life, and no matter how she came into my life, she is one of the very most important people in the world to me, and she always will be.

I met Bella as a one-year-old, and Bryson was six when I came into his life. Of course there are many differences between what you do with a one-year-old and a six-year-old. There are different activities that seem to interest most boys versus the activities that seem to interest most girls, also, but there is one thing that I did with both of them that is kind of goofy. There is this song that I would sing to them, and they both know it; it's called "Chicery Chick". It's a song from the 60s by Sammy Kaye and Billy Williams, and here are the lyrics below:

> *"Once there lived a chicken who would say "chick-chick"*
> *"Chick-chick" all day*
> *Soon that chick got sick and tired of just "chick-chick"*
> *So, one morning he started to say:*
> *"Chickery-chick, cha-la, cha-la*
> *Check-a-la romey in a bananika*
> *Bollika, wollika, can't you see*
> *Chickery chick is me?"*
> *Every time you're sick and tired of just the same old thing*
> *Sayin' just the same old words all day*
> *Be just like the chicken who found something new to sing*
> *Open up your mouth and start to say*
> *Oh!*
> *"Chickery-chick, cha-la, cha-la*
> *Check-a-la romey in a bananika*
> *Bollika, wollika, can't you see*
> *Chickery chick is me?"*

If you pull up this song on YouTube, you'll see these ladies in their dresses on stage singing this song with the most bizarre lyrics you could ever here. Both of my kids know this song,

171

and when they were little, they'd sometimes sing it in public, and people would look at us strangely. They were probably thinking, what odd language is this kid speaking? But we've had so much fun with it, and they know it by heart. I'm sure they'll teach it to their kids too one day.

Bella, especially, brings this and everything she does to life with her special flair and heart, and she's very willful. She has a personality that will light up a room; she has the power to change a space just by being in it. We share this silly, creative sense of humor, and we'll create these videos—we'll go on for about 45 minutes doing this, making up stories. Then we'd start dancing and being goofy, and it's the best time!

On top of her creativity, brilliance, willfulness and joy, Bella is fearless! She has been known to take her imagination and creativity a little over the top at school, enrolling everyone into her creative stories, whether they are real or imagined, not wanting to ever stop the play. She puts 100% into everything, when she's cheering or singing or just being her spirited creative self, and her joy always makes me smile.

Bella, it is an honor to be a part of your life. To see you grow up and become the little girl that you've become, and I look forward to standing by your side as you grow into a young lady with goals and dreams, achievements and some disappointments of your own. I hope that I've brought you some kind of happiness, love and support and that I continue to be that person for you. I also hope that along the way you've learned something from me. As you grow, I hope that it helps you to become the person that you want to be, the version of you that you know you can be.

Bella, you've helped me to see the world with wonder again as you experience it for the first time with all of its magic.

172

Things like flowers and the sky, birds and trees, exploring the simplest of things with you become giant adventures as you grow and understand the world. Your spirited willfulness might get you into a little trouble now, but it is sure to take you very far as you learn to use its power.

In time, you'll learn how to reign in that massive power you have of creativity and imagination and to channel it in the most amazing ways. In doing so, please be sure to never, ever, ever snuff out that flame inside of you. Treasure it and nurture it so that it grows in the most beautiful ways for you.

CHAPTER 14: Living Happily Ever After?

Dreams Coming True

What would happen if all your dreams came true?

It's an interesting idea to ponder—all the success, the love, the family, the personal development, the good health, the great body, the home, the stuff, the experiences, the spirituality—everything you could possibly dream. What would your life be like?

Then what would you do? Possibly you could embark on some philanthropic mission, dedicating your life to helping and uplifting others and that would be great! For me, personally, I believe that the journey and the struggle through the journey has purpose and rewards far greater than the actual achievement of them. It's those parts where I've learned and grown the most and that have allowed me to become a better version of myself. Yet, I wouldn't reject having all of my dreams granted! Bring it… I'd find new challenges, bigger dreams and more fantastic goals to achieve.

One great dream of mine has come true—you are reading my book. To each of you who have entrusted me with your attention by reading this, I'm so deeply honored that you chose to take your incredibly valuable and precious time spending it with me and my words. I'm humbled and incredibly blessed by you. It means more to me than you will ever know. Throughout the creation of this book, the telling of these stories, extracting lessons learned and teachable moments to gift to you, my life continues to be blessed.

Throughout the chapters, and in one particular chapter, I mentioned a relationship—a marriage—to an amazing woman that took an excruciatingly painful turn. To me, we seemed to have the ideal relationship from the start with similar goals and values. We had plans of building a powerful and empowering business together, raising her daughter together and growing in our life together. Then, things took a horrible turn. Our relationship turned toxic, like a delicious poison that we both kept drinking, until we were too drunk in it to see what we were doing to each other and ourselves. When the relationship finally ended, I thought for a while that it might have destroyed me; I was broken and hollow—

just a shell of who I used to be. I saw nothing good left, just a worthless, unredeemable emptiness.

In fact, the opposite happened. It led me on the greatest most powerful path of personal development and spiritual growth beyond anything that I could have ever dreamed. And, while my relationship with my wife was over, I remained close to her daughter—the bond between Bella and me has always been one of the most special connections I have ever had in my life, and I'm forever grateful that no matter how painful my relationship with Bella's mother became, she always wanted me to be a positive light in Bella's life. As I mentioned before, Bella's dad is a strong presence for Bella, and he loves her very much. So, unlike my relationship with Bryson, my son, where I am his only real father figure, Bella is blessed to have two men in her life who love her and are there for her.

Renewed Relationship

Then in the most astonishing turn of events, not only have I reconciled with my wife, we are 100% back together as a couple! It was a slow and cautious road. I knew that I needed to like her again. We needed to reconcile as friends and enjoy, trust and look forward to being together again in a completely different type of relationship than the one we had before. Lessons of forgiveness, redemption and reconciliation took on a deeper meaning than I had ever thought possible, particularly with this relationship. In fact, if you had asked me one year ago if we would ever be a couple again, I would have exclaimed, "Absolutely not, no, never!" I'm overjoyed to say that through an incredible amount of healing that both of us had to undertake, we seem to have the relationship now that I always dreamed we would have so many years ago.

We had to grow apart before we could grow together it seems. Recently, I was asked what the difference is now compared to then, and it's a simply understanding the personal growth we each worked on individually that has allowed us to come back together as two whole persons who support one another versus two broken people attempting to become whole separate from one another. When you're broken and someone starts tearing away at your wounds, you'll never heal. Then you begin tearing away at their wounds in retaliation—you end up in a vicious circle of mutually assured destruction. There's no way that we could have developed a healthy relationship like that. We could have attended couples counseling every day for 15 years, and it wouldn't have stopped this destructive dance we had going. We absolutely could not have grown into the people we are today if we attempted to do it together—we became committed to tearing each other down daily.

Now, through time apart spent healing our own wounds, understanding our own issues and dedicating ourselves to positive growth and daily mindset adjustments for our own growth and well-being, we've abandoned the impulse to lash out, to tear down and to allow others to treat us that way. Through personal growth, developing and respecting personal boundaries becomes natural, and a focus on compassion, kindness and support becomes your first priority. You'll notice that it becomes easier over time to not allow negative moments of anger, confusion and discord to hold space and linger for very long. We prioritize closeness, being playful and enjoying one another while also picking up where we left off as best as possible, building our lives together again.

Forgiveness

What does it mean to forgive someone, exactly? So many people have written books and passages on the subject. Holy Scriptures address the importance of forgiveness countless times—as a means of character, holiness, redemption and healing. We long for forgiveness of our sins, indiscretions, actions and inactions that have caused harm or mistrust in others. We often struggle to forgive ourselves most of all, and we allow these painful memories from our past—accurate and inaccurate—to haunt our thoughts and dreams, to disturb our peace of mind and spirit. So, how do we forgive?

178

What I find very odd is that often if you seek out an answer to that question, you are usually met with platitudes and loosely associated responses: we can forgive but not forget; forgiveness is a gift that we give to ourselves; it doesn't mean that we now like the person—we just take the power of the harm they did to us away, etc.

Absolutely none of that tells you how to go about forgiving. So, how do you do it? The short answer is, I have no idea. For me, it has always shown up differently, and it depends on the person and my relationship with them, the problem that is being forgiven and the likelihood that it will be repeated and/or can it be mended, the pain I experienced, my mindset at the time, my connection to my faith and a whole host of other factors weighing into it.

My frame of reference begins with the teachings of Jesus Christ, and the process of forgiveness through those teachings has everything to do with empathy and compassion. Christ had unwavering empathy and compassion for us which led Him to forgive all of our sins as described in the scriptures. The process of forgiveness begins when you look inside your heart to the anger, resentment and pain and choose to release it. The path to doing this is empathy and compassion—making an effort to understand the other (or yourself) as a whole human, worthy of love and kindness, not just the action or inaction that caused harm.

To put it in purely secular terms, the "how" is the profound recognition of the other person's humanity, which is the same humanity that you have, I have—that we each possess. Then, we must go within ourselves to forgive another, often seeing that the other person is merely a mirror of the anger, resentment and pain we feel towards ourselves. This makes the act of forgiveness even more healing and cleansing than we ever believed it could.

In my relationship with my wife, reconciliation was only possible through mutual forgiveness and mutual empathy and compassion. Of course, forgiveness doesn't always lead to reconciliation, nor should it. In relationships that are irreparably toxic, harmful, abusive or even irreparably careless, reconciliation isn't likely. Yet,

179

forgiveness is always possible. I know that there are certain deeds that most might deem unforgivable, such as murder or child abuse, but I promise you that somewhere, someone has forgiven another for that very deed you feel can't or shouldn't be forgiven as impossible as it may seem.

The process of forgiveness also includes complete honesty—to truly forgive you must reach a point of unusual honesty about the situation which includes facing all of the factors involved. This leads to open-mindedness where you are willing to abandon your rigid views of the situation which is where empathy and compassion enter. Willingness—you must also be willing to forgive, willing to release your hold on your anger, resentment and pain which might be more difficult than it seems. We often don't realize how addicted we can get to harboring ill-will against others. That resentment can feel powerful, protective and purposeful—even righteous—which is absolutely false, but it can feel so important. These are highly damaging illusions that can keep us stuck in despair and unwilling to forgive.

Honesty can also be challenging because to be truly honest, we often need to confront any part we might have played in the issue. That's not always the case, but often it is. Then by looking at others through a lens of compassion and empathy, we often find that we have a list of apologies and "making amends" that need to occur on our end as well. Being humble is the answer here; acknowledging that we have our own transgressions that need to be forgiven and acknowledging the many times we've been bestowed the gift of forgiveness by those around us helps to soften our hearts and open them up to forgive others.

Now, we enter into the part where we can discuss the why of forgiveness. We forgive others and ourselves so that we aren't held captive emotionally and psychologically by our past. We let go of the baggage weighing us down, and we enter anew into a space of honesty, integrity, empathy and compassion. We heal.

Forging a New Relationship

Relationships fall apart often—marriages, friendships, siblings, parents and children, etc. Sometimes they end for a while then pick back up. Other times, they end permanently. Then at times, they are too complex to end permanently even if you want them to, such as when children are involved, joint businesses, family, or shared assets, etc. No matter the totality of the dynamics, when you do reconcile a relationship, it can get a little messy at times. Forgiveness is a real issue, but let's say that you've moved past that, at least at some level. Are children involved? Are you co-parenting? Are others meddling in your relationship such as other family members and friends or spouses/significant others? Do you have to make joint decisions on finances and business? Or, do you both just miss having a relationship with one another and you want to explore a potential new way to make it work with healthier boundaries and mutual respect that you were both lacking previously?

Whatever specific type of reconciliation you might be facing, just know that somewhere out there, someone else has done it successfully before you. If you are both committed to a positive outcome, there absolutely is hope. It's far from a guarantee, but if you are both on the same page about trying to make it work, it is possible. In my reconciliation with my wife, as I mentioned previously, I needed to see if I could actually "like" her again—to see if we could be good friends. The moment that happened, everything clicked for me, and a full reconciliation was in motion! Of course, she needed to be onboard with this, too, with the same level of commitment, desire and goals. Together, and only together, have we been able to create a successful reconciliation of our marriage.

Next Level Motivators

An important part of this growth together also includes our commitment to building our business together. This includes my wife and my business partner Dora who has been with me from the beginning, inspiring and coaching others to become the best versions of themselves daily.

Through all that you've experienced in this book, if you find that my stories, what insight I have offered and what action steps I've recommended have had an impact on you, I humbly invite you to reach out to me directly. I'm available for coaching, speaking engagements—live and virtually—and I am so blessed to have had the opportunity to share this book with you.

We are a team of three at the moment, building this business from the bottom of our hearts, wanting the very best for everyone we are privileged to have contact with, and we are so grateful and excited that we get to do this for a living. Nothing means more to me than to be a conduit to the healing and empowerment of others, so that they may be the best versions of themselves. *Blessed and Unstoppable!*

AFTERWORD

by Daphne Taylor Street

I am deeply honored to have had the opportunity to produce this book with John Hunter. He has an extraordinary spirit and a purpose-driven mission that jumps off these pages and captures readers in a palpable way. With compelling storytelling matched with life lessons, John has provided a work that will appeal to all audiences seeking to level-up their lives, no matter how stuck or dire their situation might seem at the moment.

The creation of this book was not without its challenges. Beginning with ambitious goals, a global pandemic, and all the chaos and stress that came with it, did its best to create delays, conflicts, and barriers. Meanwhile, John's personal life shifted while we were creating this book leading to heart-warming changes that we've included here. Nevertheless, we persevered!

Readers will find that this book is not just a collection of life stories and self-help tips, but it is a "slice of life" from a man who has done the work and walked the walk, carefully examining his own life and life lessons that he has mapped out in this book. I'm proud to have been a part of its development.

About the Editor and Publisher

Daphne Taylor Street, founder of Street Media and Publishing, LLC.

With more than 20 years of professional writing and editing experience and 10s of millions of dollars' worth of proposals and contracts to her credit, Daphne has taken a deep dive into the publishing world with 21st Century knowledge and strategies.

Daphne is an international bestselling author, editor in chief and producer of the former Forbes Living magazine, is widely published in national and regional magazines, professional award-winning blogs and bestselling books as a writer, co-author, editor, and ghost writer, *but shhhh… we can't talk about the ghosts!*

For more information, visit:
www.StreetMediaandPublishing.com

www.ingramcontent.com/pod-product-compliance
Lightning Source LLC
LaVergne TN
LVHW051345080426
835509LV00020BA/3294